GW00362667

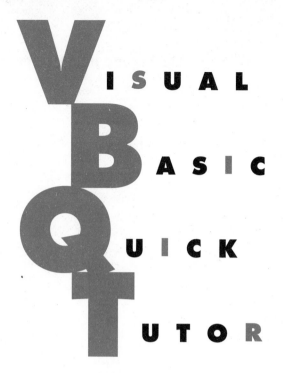

VISUAL BASIC QUICK TUTOR

BY ROBERT M. SMYTHE

boyd & fraser publishing company

I(T)P An International Thomson Publishing Company

Danvers • Albany • Bonn • Boston • Cincinnati • Detroit • London • Madrid • Melbourne
Mexico City • New York • Paris • San Francisco • Singapore • Tokyo • Toronto • Washington

To my wonderful wife, Sue, and terrific children, Debbie and Jillian

Production Manager: Patty Stephan
Production Editor: Jean Bermingham
Composition: Gex, Inc.
Interior Design: Barbara M. Libby
Cover Design: Diana Coe
Manufacturing Coordinator: Brian Harvey

bf © 1996 by boyd & fraser publishing company
A division of International Thomson Publishing Inc.

I(T)P   The ITP™ logo is a trademark under license.

Printed in the United States of America

For more information, contact boyd & fraser publishing company:

boyd & fraser publishing company
One Corporate Place • Ferncroft Village
Danvers, Massachusetts 01923, USA

International Thomson Publishing Europe
Berkshire House 168-173
High Holborn
London WCIV 7AA, England

Thomas Nelson Australia
102 Dodds Street
South Melbourne 3205
Victoria, Australia

Nelson Canada
1120 Birchmount Road
Scarborough, Ontario
Canada M1K 5G4

International Thomson Editores
Campose Eliseos 385, Piso 7
Col. Polanco
11560 Mexico D.F. Mexico

International Thomson Publishing GmbH
Konigswinterer Strasse 418
53227 Bonn, Germany

International Thomson Publishing Asia
221 Henderson Road
#05-10 Henderson Building
Singapore 0315

International Thomson Publishing Japan
Hirakawacho Kyowa Building, 3F
2-2-1 Hirakawacho
Chiyoda-ku, Tokyo 102, Japan

All rights reserved. No part of this work may be reproduced or used in any form or by any means—graphic, electronic, or mechanical, including photocopying, recording, taping, or information storage and retrieval systems—without written permission from the publisher.

Names of all products mentioned herein are used for identification purposes only and may be trademarks and/or registered trademarks of their respective owners. boyd & fraser publishing company disclaims any affiliation, association, or connection with, or sponsorship or endorsement by such owners.

1 2 3 4 5 6 7 8 9 10 BN 9 8 7 6 5

ISBN: 0-7895-0016-7

Contents

Contents, cont.

Contents, cont.

Contents, cont.

Contents, cont.

Contents, cont.

Contents, cont.

ontents, cont.

Preface

One of the fastest growing programming languages for Windows is Microsoft's Visual Basic. More than a language, Visual Basic is a comprehensive program development environment. You can now use Visual Basic to write procedures for other applications, such as Access and Excel. Yet learning to use Visual Basic is simple and fun.

The Visual Basic Quick Tutor is designed to help you learn Visual Basic quickly. From the very first chapter you will be writing full Windows programs: applications with all the features you expect of Windows programs, such as overlapping, sizable windows, scroll bars, pulldown menus, and minimize buttons. Sit down beside your computer, start reading, and begin making Windows applications.

The BASIC Story

In 1963, John Kemeny and Thomas Kurtz created the Beginners All-purpose Symbolic Instruction Code (BASIC). Incorporated as a resident language in such early microcomputers as the Commodore PET and Apple II, BASIC quickly achieved the reputation of being easy to learn. However, BASIC was not regarded as being for "serious" programmers, who preferred assembly language or compiled programs written in Pascal and, later, C.

One objection was BASIC's slowness. A computer had to translate each BASIC statement into the machine's language at run time. If a program required that the computer execute a particular statement twice, the computer had to translate, or interpret, the same statement twice. Another criticism was Basic's lack of structure. It was easy to write unstructured, branching, twisting, "spaghetti" code. The versions of BASIC available on early microcomputers did not provide subprograms (which allow local variables) and demanded the use of the GOTO statement.

Although some structured BASIC implementations appeared, such as CPM-BASIC, GW-BASIC, Better BASIC, and Waterloo BASIC, the language kept its reputation of being for beginners only. In 1982, Microsoft released QuickBASIC. Although not forbidding the use of GOTO statements, QuickBASIC was easy to use, provided a wealth of programming structures, and was fast. These advantages drew second looks from programmers. Software companies began marketing libraries of sophisticated QuickBASIC routines, and QuickBASIC columns sprung up in computer magazines. QuickBASIC had the best of both worlds: it precompiled each line as it was entered and therefore was fast, but its programs behaved like interpreted programs, enabling the programmer to run, stop, alter, and continue them. You could make the final version of a QuickBASIC program into a stand-alone .EXE file. QBasic, a subset of QuickBASIC, comes with DOS 5.0.

A year after releasing Windows, Microsoft announced the introduction of Visual Basic. This language is a form of QuickBASIC that contains built-in Windows structures, such as pulldown menus, buttons, and mouse routines. Visual Basic took off, according to Tom Button of Microsoft: "In just the first year since Visual Basic for Windows was released, hundreds of thousands of developers have adopted Visual Basic for their application development and shipped over 4 million copies of Visual Basic applications to end users."[1]

Microsoft has now released Visual Basic for Windows 3.0, as well as Visual Basic for MS-DOS. You can link the newest version of Excel (Microsoft's top-of-the-line spreadsheet) to a Visual Basic application. This book helps you learn how to use Visual Basic for Windows (version 1, 2, or 3). As you progress through the book, you will be amazed at how easily and quickly you can produce professional-looking Windows applications.

Using The Visual Basic Quick Tutor

To the student

This book is designed to help you learn to make Windows programs quickly in Microsoft's new language, Visual Basic.

You don't learn to program computers by reading about or listening to a teacher talk about programming. You learn by making programs. In the early days of personal computers, computer magazines contained small programs that the reader could enter and then modify. *The Visual Basic Quick Tutor* is based on the fact that the best way to learn Visual Basic is to begin using it. The book consists of lessons. You don't read the lessons, you *do* them, at your computer.

Each chapter starts with several introductory notes about concepts that will arise in the application program that you will develop in the lesson. Some involve reading, and some involve some Visual Basic procedures that you enter on the keyboard. In each chapter, you create a Visual Basic application, a program. This tutorial lesson teaches you several interesting features or techniques. The **Instructions** section tells you how to set up the program and what to type, and also explains how the program works. The **Modifications** section contains some suggestions for modifying the program. *Try them.* Typing in the code and verifying that it works will help you learn. But figuring out how to change the code to make it do something else will help you learn even faster. Some chapters have an **Enhancements** section, inviting you to try some more challenging modifications.

Each chapter ends with a short Exercises section. This consists of some review questions about concepts introduced in the lessons and one or two short programs to try.

This book includes a disk that contains all the applications you can make in the lessons. You should use the programs only to see a suggested final appearance for the application or to observe what the program does. You will learn more by creating the programs yourself, not by just examining them. Try to resist the temptation to load every program just to save yourself some typing.

---

[1]Preface to the pamphlet *Companion Products and Services Directory for Visual Basic for MS-DOS* (Summer 1992, Tom Button, Group Product Manager and Visual Basic Programmer, Applications Programmability Group, Microsoft Corporation).

The *Visual Basic Quick Tutor* is not an in-depth study of specific Visual Basic commands. For that, you can consult the manual. But you will make real Windows applications while learning the most important techniques. You must be willing to think, though. For example, when this book does not give you complete information about what a certain statement does, run the program with and without the statement. Ask yourself what difference the statement makes.

The most important thing to realize as you begin using this book is that you develop programming skill *by programming*, by experimentation, by trying to accomplish a task in various ways.

If you follow through the *Visual Basic Quick Tutor*, typing as you read and thinking as you type, you will learn to develop Windows applications efficiently.

To the instructor

The philosophy of the *Visual Basic Quick Tutor* is that students learn better by trying than by just reading, by doing than by just listening.

The main portion of each chapter is an application program that the students are to create at their computer. They are to type the code for the application, reading the text's explanations about what the statements do. Although students will certainly ask you what a given line does, and you can answer, try to encourage them to figure it out. Tell them to omit a line and see what change results. Suggest that they put a STOP (or toggle a breakpoint) before and after the line and then run the program. If the line is something like Text1.Enabled = **True**, tell them to change the setting to **False** and compare the results.

Encourage students to make their own modifications. If you are evaluating them by noting when they have finished each program, demand a slight change before accepting the program as complete. For example, if in the finished application a message box is to contain an exclamation mark and Yes and No buttons, have the student demonstrate that the box comes up as required. Congratulate the student, but then ask to see the box with a stop sign and OK and Cancel buttons instead.

This book expects your students to be able to think. The book begins with explicit instructions:

Enter the following in Sub ExitButton_Click:

```
Sub ExitButton_Click ()
        End
End Sub
```

But in later chapters, students might read the following:

Don't forget to code your Exit button.

Thereafter, the book might not even refer to the ExitButton that appears on the picture of the form.

By all means, present material to your students and answer their questions. But, in keeping with the spirit of the *Visual Basic Quick Tutor*, encourage your students to be creative and to think for themselves.

Acknowledgements

I would like to thank the staff of boyd & fraser for taking on this project and helping me carry it through to completion. Thanks to Carol Crowell, Publishing Process Director; Rita Ferrandino, Acquisitions Editor; Jean Bermingham, Production Editor; Shelly Langman and Jerry Ralya, Development Editors; and Andy Saff, copyeditor. Thanks also to the following reviewers who provided useful feedback and suggestions:

Juan A. Henriques   Grantham College
Rajiv Malken   LaMar University at Orange
Priscilla McGill   Rogue Community College
Charles M. Williams   Georgia State University

A special thank you goes to my students who, over several years and grades, field-tested the chapters.

Rob Smythe

Chapter 1

Designing a Visual Basic Application

Visual Basic is a programming environment. With Visual Basic, you create programs that you or anyone else can use. In this chapter, you learn the fundamental concepts of working with Visual Basic and design a simple program.

1.1 What is programming?

Few computer users are programmers; most are program users. A program, or computer application, is software that the user runs on the computer to perform a task. Examples of popular computer applications are word processors, spreadsheets, paint programs, and games. These applications are programs that someone else, a computer *programmer*, has created.

Figure 1.1 shows an application program that enables a user to create word-search puzzles. The user has entered a title for the puzzle, has checked some printing options, and is about to press a button.

	Word Search	
	Title for Puzzle Holiday Words	
	Instructions	
Edit the Words	All words placed. You can Display or Print the Puzzle now.	Print the Puzzle
Make the Puzzle	☒ Print Answer Page ☒ Print list of words	Load new Words
Display the Puzzle		Save the Words
	Quit	

Figure 1.1
Controls on a form

A typical application program provides one or more screens or windows (called *forms* by Visual Basic) that contain menus, buttons, or words. The screen prompts the user to click the mouse button or enter a response on the keyboard. The program then performs some task such as calculating an answer, retrieving data, or manipulating some text. Usually the user will see the result of the action. For example, an answer to a calculation might appear in red printing, a game piece might move from one square to the next, or the screen might change color.

But how does a button click actually cause something to happen on the screen? The *programmer*, the creator of the application, writes the instructions that tell the computer what to do, and how to do it, when the user takes an action.

Consider any computer application that you use[–]a word processor, a spreadsheet, a paint program, or a game. All are similar in that each shows the user a screen that contains some printing, some buttons, a menu, or some other request for his or her response. After the user takes an action, the application *does something*. It might beep, clear the screen, display a title, or take some other action.

Your job as programmer is to create the display that the user sees, and to write the *code* that makes the application (the program) do what you (and the user) want it to do.

1.2 Programming with Visual Basic

When you create programs with Visual Basic, you decide how the screen is to appear to the user, which actions to allow the user to perform, and what is to result from these actions (that is, what calculations the computer will perform and what the user is to see on the screen). Your programs will be Windows applications, so they will run in one or more windows, or *forms*. Each form will contain several *controls*, such as buttons, message boxes, or scroll bars. You set initial *properties* for the controls, such as the color of a label or the caption on a button. Each control has several *events* that can happen to it. For example, the user can click or double-click a button or modify the contents of a text box. By writing Visual Basic *code*, you give the computer instructions telling it what to do when each significant event occurs.

The following sections describe these steps in more detail.

Place controls on the form

Visual Basic is an object-oriented, event-driven language that you can use to develop programs that run under Microsoft Windows. When you create a program, you design one or more *forms*, which are windows that open when the user runs your program. On the forms you place objects, called *controls*. Controls enable the program's user to enter information, select commands from pulldown menus, or otherwise initiate activity.

Figure 1.2 shows the form that opens when you are about to print a document from Microsoft Word. The form contains many controls. On the right are command buttons (OK, Cancel, and so on), each with a different *caption* or title. At the top, beside the *label* Print What, is a *combo* box. When you click on the combo box's arrow, a menu drops down from which you can make a selection. A second combo box is open at the bottom. The Page Range *frame* contains *option buttons* and a *text box* in which you can enter page numbers. The frame also contains a label in a smaller font, which presents some instructions for the user. Other labels are used for the printer name, and the words Printer:, Copies:, and Print:. At the bottom right are *check boxes* (Print to File and Collate Copies) that enable the user to set print options. Finally, a text box and a tiny vertical *scroll bar* enable the user to select the number of copies to print.

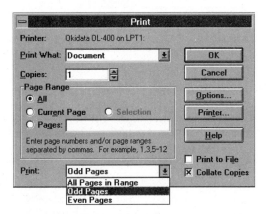

Figure 1.2
Controls on a form

You undoubtedly are familiar with the *menu* bar that appears across the top of almost all Windows applications. Each choice on a menu, and each choice on any submenu that drops down from the menu, is a control. In Figure 1.3, the Settings menu from Clock (a program that comes with Windows in the Accessories group) has dropped down, after the user clicked on it with the mouse. Visual Basic enables you to design such structured menus easily.

Figure 1.3
A drop-down menu

The form itself is a control that the user can move or resize. It comes with the standard window control button (at the top left) and maximize and minimize buttons (at the top right).

In Figure 1.4, you should be able to find option buttons, a check box, command buttons, and a horizontal scroll bar.

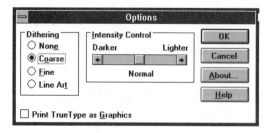

Figure 1.4
More controls on a form

The controls that you can place on your applications are found in the *toolbox*, which is one of the windows on the Visual Basic design screen.

Give each control a name

Each control that you place on a form must have a unique name. When you place a new control on a form, Visual Basic gives it a *default* name[–]an initial, conventional name. Examples are Command1 for the first button, Combo1 for the first menu box, Option2 for the second option button, and so on. You should rename most controls to give them more meaningful names. For example, if the *caption*, the text on the face of a button, is OK, you might refer to the button as OKbutton. Look again at Figure 1.4 and identify the controls that the programmer might have named TTbox, Course, AboutButton, and Intensity.

The form itself also has a name. The form in Figure 1.4 could have been named PrintOptions, for example.

Set each control's properties

Each control has associated *properties*. For example, some properties of a command button are Caption, position (Left and Top), and size (Width and Height). A text box's properties include its foreground and background colors, its Text (that is, the box's contents), the font size of the text, and whether the text box has scroll bars. An option button will have a value, **True** or **False**, depending on whether the user has selected it. You will quickly learn to set the important properties of most of the common controls.

When you write code for your program, you refer to the control's properties by specifying the name of the control, *followed by a dot* (or period), then the property. The following are valid expressions for defining the names and properties of several controls shown in Figure 1.4:

OKbutton.Caption	The control name is OKbutton, the property is *Caption*
NoneOption.Value	The control name is NoneOption, the property is Value
Intensity.Max	The control name is Intensity, the property is the scroll bar's maximum value

The following are examples of Visual Basic statements that set properties. (You learn to write Visual Basic code when you create the practical application later in this chapter.)

```
Quitbutton.Caption = "End"
Textbox1.Text = ""                      'erase the text
Titlebox.Caption = "Inventory Control"
Form2.Show = True
Namelabel.FontSize = 24
Addbutton.Visible = False
```

The preceding statements set properties while the program is running. You select all the initial properties by making selections from pulldown menus or by dragging the mouse. For example, to set the button's position (Top and Left) and size (Height and Width), you can grab it with the mouse, drag it to the desired location, and stretch it as if it were a frame in a word processor or a rectangle in a paint program. Then you can set other properties by selecting from the provided options without having to type statements such as the preceding.

Because the form itself is a control, it has properties. Refer again to Figure 1.4. If the form is named PrintOptions, you might find a code line specifying a Caption property as follows:

```
PrintOptions.Caption = "Options"
```

Determine the events that might occur when your program runs

When running your program, the user will perform an action on a control. He or she might click a check box, double-click a command button, enter or change the text in a text box, press a key (such as Tab or Enter), or select a control from a drop-down menu. An action that takes place on a control is called an *event*. Table 1.1 shows some sample controls, actions, and the Visual Basic name for the events.

Table 1.1 Sample Visual Basic Controls and Events

Control	User Action	Event
A text box called WordBox	Enter a word into a text box	WordBox_Change
A pulldown-menu option called NewOption	Make a selection	NewOption_Click
A picture box called Picture1	Use the mouse to select a region of the picture	Picture1_DragOver
A command button called SaveButton	Double-click the button	SaveButton_DblClick

In the third column of Table 1.1, notice that you specify the event by writing the control's name (chosen by the programmer) followed by the event, separating the control name and the event *with an underscore*. Don't confuse this with the way that you specify properties, for which you separate the control's name and property with a period.

Some events can occur without the user taking any action. Examples of such events are initial actions that the program takes (such as displaying and then clearing titles) and actions that timers trigger (such as displaying a message every five minutes to remind users to save their work).

Attach Visual Basic code to each significant event

When you create your program, you write *code*, instructional statements, to tell the computer what to do when each event takes place. The programming language that comes with Visual Basic derives from the widely used BASIC programming language.

Each line of code is an *instruction*. Here are some examples:

```
A = length * width                'calculate the area
If age > 12 Then Print "You are now a teenager"
Amount = cost + tax               'add the tax
Cls                               'clear the screen
```

Instructions use key words (which you will learn as you go), arithmetic symbols, and words (variables) that you define as the program runs.

You place your code into the *Sub procedure* for the event that is to trigger it. For example, if clicking the QuitButton is to end the program, you write the single instruction End into the QuitButton_Click event, as follows:

```
Sub QuitButton_Click ()
    End              'the only line you type
End Sub
```

Study the form shown in Figure 1.5. The user enters in two text boxes values corresponding to the sides of a rectangle and then presses the Calculate button. The computer calculates and displays the area of the rectangle.

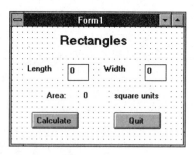

Figure 1.5
A form that calculates areas

Suppose that you named the two text boxes, which now each contain a zero, LengthBox and WidthBox. To the right of the label Area is a label that you call

AnswerBox. The code that you would write for the CalculateButton might look like the following[1]:

```
Sub CalculateButton_Click ()
    Answer.Caption = LengthBox.Text * WidthBox.Text
End Sub
```

1.3 The Visual Basic design screen

Visual Basic provides several windows and toolboxes that give you access to a variety of design controls. The following sections introduce these controls.

The Visual Basic windows

When you start Visual Basic, you see one or more windows (depending on the version that you are using). Figure 1.6 shows the Visual Basic 3.0 Design Screen with five windows open.

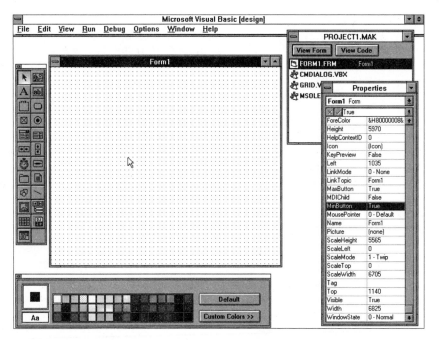

Figure 1.6
The Visual Basic design screen

---

[1]Advanced note: Better code would be

```
    Answer.Caption = Str$(Val(LengthBox.Text) * Val(WidthBox.Text))
```

Experienced BASIC programmers, or those accustomed only to Visual Basic 1.0, might be surprised that this example even works. They might be even more surprised that the following example, which is even shorter, also works:

```
    Answer = LengthBox * WidthBox
```

Visual Basic has a type of variable called Variant that can switch between string and numeric variable types. Chapter 4 provides information on variant variables.

Clockwise from the left to the bottom, the windows are the following:

Window	Description
Toolbox	This window provides a set of controls that you can include in your application. For example, the toolbox enables you to add a command button that says Quit.
Form	This window displays when your application runs. (Non-Windows programmers might think of this window as the "screen" that the user will see.) You place on the form the controls that you pick up from the toolbox. (In Figure 1.6, no controls have been placed yet.)
Project window	Your application (or program) might consist of more than one form. The project window lists each of these forms, which are saved as separate files. In Figure 1.6, the project's only form is Form1, which has a default file name Form1.frm. The project window also lists the programmer's utility subprograms that your version of Visual Basic contains.
Properties list	This window lists the properties of the selected control. When an empty form is displayed, the list consists of the properties of the form itself. Beneath the word Properties is the Object combo box, which displays a drop-down list of all controls on the form. Under that combo box is the Settings box, in which you can enter values or select a setting from the drop-down list. In Figure 1.6, Caption is highlighted, and both the Settings box and the column next to Caption display Form1. Note also that the form's title bar indicates that the form's Caption is Form1.
Color palette	This window enables you to assign colors by selecting them with the mouse instead of entering color numbers.

Another window, the code window, is not open in Figure 1.6. This window is where you enter Visual Basic instructions from the keyboard. If you were to double-click on the form, the Form_Click code window would open.

When you start Visual Basic, you might not see all these windows. The Window menu enables you display the toolbox and the project window. The project window contains a list of all forms that your program will use. If you don't see the form window, you can click the project window's View Form button.

The controls in the toolbox

Figure 1.7 shows the tools that come with Visual Basic 3.0. Except for the pointer arrow, which you use to enable your pointer on the screen, each tool represents a type of control that you can place on the forms that you design.

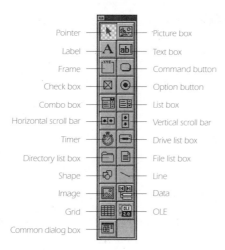

Figure 1.7
The toolbox

As you work through the applications in this book, you will learn how to use the most important of these tools.

Application 1

Creating your first Visual Basic program

Using the applications

Each chapter of this book includes an application as a tutorial lesson to do on your computer. As you work through the application, you are provided with the steps that you need to follow to create a complete Visual Basic application. While creating the application, you learn Visual Basic concepts and programming techniques. Each application has suggested modifications and enhancements that you can try to implement. Although the complete applications are contained on the disks that accompany this book, you will learn more by following the instructions yourself. By implementing the suggested modifications and enhancements, some of which you will invent yourself, you will learn Visual Basic quickly.

This first application has more detailed instructions than those in the chapters that follow. Your goal in this and all applications is to create a complete, working Windows program. When you finish, you can turn your *source code*, the written Visual Basic instructions, into an *.EXE file*, the single executable program that you can run from Windows. You save the application's source code and .EXE files on a disk.

Overview

The application begins by displaying a form that looks like Figure 1.8. When the user presses the Greeting button, your name appears on the screen. Pressing the End button closes the application.

Figure 1.8
Application 1 at run time

A Visual Basic application consists of at least two files: a file ending with the file extension .FRM for the form, and a project file with the extension .MAK. The form file contains the information about the appearance and coding associated with a form. The project file lists the forms that compose the application, which in this case is only one form.

Start Visual Basic and follow these instructions to create your application.

Instructions

Create a new project After you start Visual Basic, a blank form appears. If you don't see one, choose Project from the Window menu, point to Form1.frm in the Project window, and click the View Form button. The *default* file names for the project and form are Project1.mak and Form1.frm. A default is the initial setting that Visual Basic gives to a property. You can change the setting later. The form's default name and caption are also Form1.

Place controls on the forms Use the mouse to select from the toolbox the controls that you want to place on the form. To do so, click on a control, move your mouse to the form, and hold down the mouse button as you drag the mouse down and across the form. Figure 1.9 shows these three steps. If you have ever made a rectangle with a paint program, this click-drag-release mouse technique will be familiar. You can then resize the control or move it by dragging an edge or corner, or the entire control, to a new position on the form.

 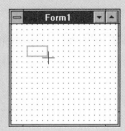 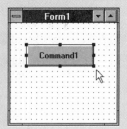

Figure 1.9
Steps for placing a button

Now begin designing the form for this application. Start by clicking on the toolbox's label tool. If the tool box is not visible, choose it from the Window menu. Move the mouse pointer near the top-left corner of your form, at the location that corresponds to the Label1 region shown in Figure 1.10. Holding down the left mouse button, drag the mouse to the bottom right; then release the button. This produces on the form a region for a label[–]a control that holds a title, message, prompt, or some other note to the user. The label's default name and caption are both Label1. You can see this by looking at the properties list beside Name and Caption. Surrounding the label are the resizing handles. By dragging a corner or a side while pressing the mouse button, you can change the label's height and width. You can move the entire label by dragging its center.

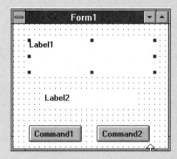

Figure 1.10
The form after you place the controls

Repeat the process to make a second, smaller label, Label2, underneath it. Then place two command buttons.

Set control properties   Click once on the Command1 button to select it. (The handles should appear around the control.) From the properties list, choose Name and replace Command1 with GreetingsButton. Select Caption and change it to Greetings. Select the second button, name it EndButton, and make its caption End.

You should always rename controls that Visual Basic has given default names. If you choose a meaningful name, one that indicates the control's function, remembering the control's name and purpose will be easier later when you write your code.

Next you set the properties for the labels. Select Label1 by clicking on it or choosing it from the Object box at the top of the properties window. Change Label1's caption by clicking on Caption and simply typing My First Windows Program. Select Alignment, click on the little arrow immediately above it to pull down the Settings box, and choose 2 (centered). Set FontSize to 13.5 and FontBold to False. Change Label's name to Title.

Now set Label2's properties. Erase the caption by choosing Caption and pressing the Backspace key. You will write code to make a caption appear while the program is running. As with Title (Label1's new name), the caption will be centered (for Alignment, select 2, centered) and in normal type (set FontBold to False). Leave the FontSize at its present value of 8. Name this label Author.

The form should now look as shown in Figure 1.11.

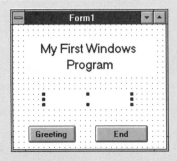

Figure 1.11
The form after you set the controls' properties

Attach code to the form or controls for each event that is to trigger some activity When you plan your program, you must decide which actions the user is to take to cause your program to do something. For example, you might have the user adjust a scroll bar to change a number in a box, or click a button to cause the words in a text box to vanish. Then you attach code to the event that is to trigger the program's response.

Your application has two buttons. By clicking the Greeting button, the user will change each label's contents. By clicking the End button, the user will end the program.

Create the code for the End button first. Double-click on the End button to open that control's code window. You will see the window shown in Figure 1.12. Enter the single command End between the Sub and End Sub lines.

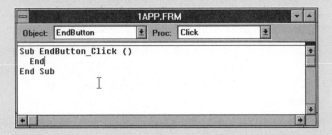

Figure 1.12
The End button's code window

You place all event routines in Sub procedures. The computer displays the first and last lines. The Object box displays EndButton, the control that you selected. (You could also select a different control from the drop-down list.) The Proc box is a drop-down list of all the actions that Visual Basic can perform on that object. The default is Click, a single click on the button. That action is the one that you want for this application. Thus the name of the event is EndButton_Click.

To display the code window for Greeting button, either double-click on the actual button or select the button from the code window's Object box. Here is the GreetingsButton code:

```
Sub GreetingsButton_Click ()
    Title.Caption = "Hello World"
```

```
        Author.Caption = "by R. Smythe" 'use your own name!
    End Sub
```

This code changes the captions in the two labels. Note that the new captions must be in quotations marks. After the apostrophe on the third line is a note to the reader of the code. The computer disregards remarks that follow apostrophes. You should include such notes to remind you what the code lines do or to explain the code line to other readers.

The *instruction set*, the list of valid Visual Basic commands and statements, is similar to that of the QBasic and QuickBasic languages that you may have seen before. (QBasic comes with DOS 5 and 6.) Visual Basic has some special instructions that make programming easier. You will learn many of these instructions by studying the examples in this book. The others you can learn about in the Help screens.

Run your program by choosing Start from the Run menu or by pressing F5. Try each button. If the program stops with an error message, you must have mistyped a line or failed to rename a control.

Save the project   From the File menu, choose Save File As. With your storage disk in drive **A**, select drive A and name the file **firstone.frm**. Then open the File menu, choose Save Project, and name it **firstone.mak**.

If this application were large, it would have run repeatedly (and you should have been saving it regularly). A complex application requires much testing and debugging. If your application does any calculations, you could try entering strange values (such as zeros and negative numbers). You would click on all controls and type ridiculous entries into text boxes. A well-designed program should survive any action that the user might take. Even though you make changes during testing, requiring you to save it repeatedly, you still should save the project before you begin serious testing. Computers sometimes "hang" (become unresponsive) when programs contain serious bugs that may appear only during rigorous testing. For this reason, you should save your program before you begin running it, especially if you have entered much code since your last save.

Create an executable file   The last step is to make your application program stand on its own, outside the Visual Basic programming environment. You create a single .EXE file to contain your program. You give the program its own icon, which you can then place at a suitable location in the Program Manager so that you can execute it at any time, without Visual Basic.

To create the .EXE file for this small program, open the File menu and choose Make .EXE File. A dialog box opens and asks you to specify a name, drive, and directory. The default directory will probably be your VB directory. To make an executable file on your disk, give the file the name a:\firstone.exe.

You can now execute the program from Windows without using Visual Basic. You probably will want to place an icon for the program in a new or existing group so that you can simply click on the icon to run the program. Creating an icon for a program is a standard Windows technique. Appendix I shows how to do this.

Modifications

1. Drag the edges of the form to make room for a third label. Instead of having the "Hello" message replace the My First Windows Program, have the message appear in the third label.

2. Add a third button with the caption By ..... Make sure that only your name appears when you press this new button.

3. Change the form's caption to something more descriptive.

Enhancements

1. Replace the End statement in Sub EndButton_Click with the following statement:

```
If MsgBox ("Are you sure", 36, "Leave Program") = 6 ⇒
then End
```

Run your program to see what results. Look up MsgBox in the Help screens to see how that command works.

2. See Appendix I for instructions for creating an icon for your program on your Windows desktop. Then exit Visual Basic and check whether your new application runs. (Don't exit from Windows, though, because you have created a Windows program, not a DOS program.)

Exercises

At your desk

1. List the types of controls that you placed on the form in Application 1. What are the names of each control?

2. Which property do you use to center a label's contents?

3. As applied to a control's property, what does the term *default* mean? What is the default font size for labels?

At your computer

Create a form with the buttons Name, Address, and Phone. Add a label that displays your name, address, or phone number when you press the appropriate button.

Chapter 2 Using Labels, Buttons, and Boxes

You learned much in Chapter 1. In Application 1, you created a small program that contains a button and a label. In this chapter, you review the concepts of controls, properties, and events. You then create an application that asks the user for data and displays it in several ways.

2.1 Setting the form's properties

When any Windows application starts, a form (see Figure 2-1) opens on the screen, either filling the entire screen or filling a window that appears over top of your current screen.

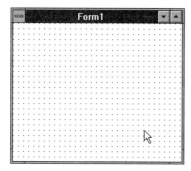

Figure 2-1
An empty form

Like any window, your form has the standard buttons: the control menu box on the top left, and minimize and maximize buttons on the top right. Although a form icon does not appear on the toolbox, the form is itself a control. Like all controls, the form has properties.

Across the title bar is the form's caption. When you start Visual Basic, the empty form's default caption is Form1. You usually begin creating an application by changing this caption. For example, you might rename the caption for the starting form of a financial program Mortgage Scheduler 1.0.

To change the form's caption, you alter a setting on the form's properties list. Figure 2-2 shows the Properties window displaying the form's properties. You can see the properties of another control on your form by selecting it from the Object box at the top (now showing Form1) or by clicking on the actual control in the form. To change the form's caption, scroll down to, or click on, Caption. Then enter the new title at the top of the Settings box.

Figure 2-2
A portion of the form's properties list

Do not confuse Caption with Name. The form's Name is the single word by which you refer to the form in your coding. For example, you could change the name for the form in Figure 2-2 (also Form1, by default) to **Mort1** by scrolling down the list of properties until you reach Name and then entering **Mort1** in the Settings box.

Finally, when you save the form, you give it a standard DOS file name, such as **MORTGAGE.FRM**. You must keep these three different "names" clear in your mind: the caption appears on the form's title bar, the name appears in your coding, and the file name on your disk.

You usually alter the form's height, width, top side, and left side with the mouse, but you can also do so by typing values into the properties list. Later chapters demonstrate how to write code to change these properties when the program is running.

You might also set other properties in the list. For example, in the running form shown in Figure 2-3, the Border was changed to 1 (fixed single), the Maxbutton to False, and the Minbutton to False. The result is a form that the user cannot resize (stretch), maximize, or minimize.

Figure 2-3
A form at run time

2.2 Designing the form

The form in Figure 2-3 has no controls, except for the standard control box in the upper-left corner. This control enables the user to move or close the application. When you create your applications, you must consider which controls to use. Do you want the user to trigger some action by clicking a button? Do you want to provide a box in which the user is to enter some data? Do you want to have a pull-down menu across the top? When designing the form, you can be creative. Do you want buttons down the side or across the bottom? Do you want to use a colored title?

In Chapter 3, you learn how to create menus across the top of the form. Buttons and text boxes are examples of controls that you can select from the toolbox, place on the form, and then move and resize with the mouse. Figure 2-4 shows the Mort1 form at a later stage of design. The form has been expanded and contains, from left to right, labels, text boxes, option buttons, check boxes, and two command buttons. The option buttons and check boxes have been placed in *frames*, to show that they operate as a unit. The frame is a control that you can name, color, size, and position. When you move the frame, the controls inside the frame move with it.

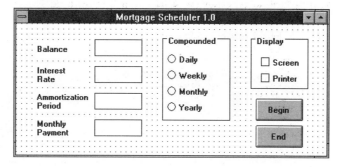

Figure 2-4
A form with many controls

The goal of the *Mortgage Scheduler 1.0* application is to enable the user to display or print tables that show the balance owed on a loan. The user enters the loan's details in the text boxes on the left, selects one of the Compounded option buttons, and chooses how to display the output: on-screen, on hard copy, or both. When the user presses the Begin button, the application performs the appropriate calculations and displays the results. The user can quit by clicking on the End button.

Of course, just designing the form is not sufficient. Unseen by the user, awaiting some action by the user on your controls, is the code that you must write to process the user's input into the desired output.

2.3 Writing the code for your controls

Your application program will usually do several things. It might calculate answers, change or erase text, display pictures on the screen, send information to the printer, or end. When you write your program, for each task you want the computer to do, you always must ask yourself this question: *What event is to cause the computer to begin its task?* For example, if a picture is to appear in the form, you must determine which control will cause the picture to appear.

For now, you need not understand how the mortgage scheduler application in Figure 2-4 computes its answer. But suppose that when the program runs, the user fills in the top three text boxes and clicks the Begin button. The application then performs a calculation and enters the result in the Monthly Payment text box. But where do you put the code for the calculation procedure?

Because the user initiates the application's action by clicking the Begin button, the appropriate place to put the instructions for calculating monthly payment is in Sub BeginButton_Click.

To cause the application to terminate, the user clicks the End button. To write the code for this event, you double-click on the End button. This displays the window shown in Figure 2-5. The window shows that the button has been suitably named Endbutton. You enter the Visual Basic command **End** at the cursor and close the window. Now, when you run the program, you can close the application by clicking the End button.

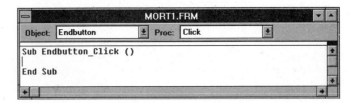

Figure 2-5
The Endbutton's subprocedure code window

| **Application 2** | **G**etting input from the user |

Overview

This application enables the user to enter some information in a text box and then clear the box by pressing a button.

Learning Objectives

- placing controls on a form
- clearing a text box
- changing fonts

- processing the data in a text box
- changing the form title

Instructions

Figure 2-6 shows the form that you need to create. The form has four labels, two text boxes, and three command buttons. To create the title, click on the toolbox's label icon, place your mouse arrow on the form, press the mouse button, and drag the label's lower-right corner down to the right. You also use this technique for the text boxes and the command buttons. You can resize a control by clicking on it to select it and then dragging a side or corner to a new location. To move a control, drag the center to another location.

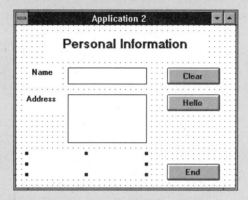

Figure 2-6
Application 2 at design time

Labels are used for titles, messages, and prompts–screen text that the user cannot change. Three of the labels have captions: Personal Information, Name, and Address. The fourth is empty; you can see where it is by the dots missing from the form background. (None of the dots show when you run the application.) For the title label, you set the Alignment property to 2 (centered) and the FontSize property to 13.5.

You should always rename each control that you place on your form, giving the control a more descriptive name. You can then more easily remember its name when you write your code. In this application, the program code refers only to the bottom label. Rename it GreetingLabel. (If the title is never going to be altered while the program runs, you might leave its default name, Label1[1], as is. You will not be referring to it again, so a more descriptive name is unnecessary.)

A text box accepts the user's typed responses. Name the top text box NameBox and the bottom one AddressBox. Text boxes don't have captions; the entry is the text box's text. To empty NameBox, select Text from the properties list and then simply press Backspace to delete the name Text1. Delete AddressBox's Text too.

---

[1]Visual Basic assigns the default names in the order in which you place controls. If the title label were the third label that you took from the toolbar, its default name would be Label3.

The first button's Caption and Name are both initially Command1. After adding the buttons and setting their captions, rename them HelloButton, ClearButton, and EndButton.

Double-click on the Clear button to bring up the subprocedure for ClearButton_Click. Then enter the following:

```
Sub ClearButton_Click ()
    NameBox.text = ""         'quote-quote = nil (nothing)
    AddressBox.text = ""      'clear AddressBox
End Sub
```

After the apostrophes, enter a message, in English, explaining what the statement does. The program ignores information that follows an apostrophe. While entering these examples, you don't absolutely have to add such messages after the apostrophes, but documenting your program in this way is a highly recommended practice.

Double-click on the End button, and then enter the following:

```
Sub EndButton_Click ()
    End
End Sub
```

To change the form's caption (the heading on the title bar), select the form itself by clicking within it, find Caption in the properties list, and enter **Application 2**.

You haven't finished setting everything up yet, but you can test how it operates so far. Run the program by opening the Run menu and choosing Start or by pressing F5.

Notice that the Hello button doesn't work. This makes sense, because you didn't code for any event for that button.

Try entering a multiline address, and you'll note that you can't move down to a second line. End your program, select the AddressBox, and find the MultiLine property. Set it to **True**, run the program again, and note the difference.

Finally, you must code the Hello button. If the user presses this button, a GreetingLabel, the blank area under the address, displays a message like "Hi, Chris. Glad to know you."

In greater detail, here's how GreetingLabel works. If the word "Toni" is in the NameBox, the Hello button displays in the GreetingLabel the words "Hi, Toni. Glad to know you." Likewise, if NameBox contains "BJ Bird", the GreetingLabel should read "Hi, BJ Bird. Glad to know you." The GreetingLabel should contain the word "Hi," a comma, a space, followed by the content of NameBox, followed by a period and the sentence "Glad to know you."

Labels and buttons have captions, but text boxes have text. The content of NameBox is NameBox.Text. The content of GreetingLabel is GreetingLabel.Caption. Therefore, the correct code to produce a GreetingLabel is as follows:

```
GreetingLabel.Caption = "Hi, " + NameBox.text + ". Glad ⇒
   to know you."
```

As you type this line, pay attention to the placement of the quotation marks, periods, and commas, and the spaces around the quotation marks.

Where do you put this code? You might think that it goes in the GreetingLabel, but that's incorrect. Ask yourself which event is to cause the GreetingLabel to change. The answer is the user clicking the Hello button, so you put the code into HelloButton_Click:

```
Sub HelloButton_Click ()
   GreetingLabel.Caption = "Hi, " + NameBox.text + ⇒
   ", Glad to know you."
End Sub
```

Modifications

1. Check whether the Clear button works properly. Enter a name and an address, and then click the Hello button and then the Clear button. Add the appropriate code to the ClearButton_Click routine to clear the GreetingLabel also. (Hint: Does the GreetingLabel have a caption or a text property?)

2. Add a button that says "My name." Enter the appropriate code so that when you click the button, your name appears automatically in the NameBox. (Hint: The code will be similar to that of ClearButton_Click, except that your name will be between the quotation marks.)

Enhancements

1. Investigate AddressBox's ScrollBars property. (Click on the text box and choose ScrollBars from the properties list. Try each setting with and without the MultiLine set to **True**. Type long lines and press Enter to see the difference.)

2. If you click the Hello button after clicking the Clear button, the GreetingLabel message is improper. Perhaps the program should execute the code in the HelloButton_Click routine only if NameBox and AddressBox include text. (Hint: To check whether NameBox.text *is anything*, check that NameBox.text is *not nothing*.)[2] You will need an **If** statement, a less-than and greater-than sequence (<>), which means not equal to, and two double quotation marks (""), which means no characters.

3. To prevent the user from accidentally clearing the data, add the message "Are you sure?" See Application 1's enhancements.

---

[2]Visual Basic (and all computer languages) follow rules of logic. If you *haven't got nothing*, then *you have got something*. This conflicts with growing popular usage, where some people say "I haven't got nothing" when they mean "I haven't got anything" or "I *have* got nothing." `Namebox.text <> ""` means "Namebox.text *is* not equal to nothing," which is the same thing as saying "Namebox.text *is* equal to something." Note that there is no space between the quotation marks.

Exercises

At your desk

1.   Three of the windows that you can have open while designing your applications are the toolbox, project, and properties windows. What is the purpose of each?

2.   Distinguish among a form's name, file name, and caption. How do you set a form's file name?

3.   What are the default names for a form, a command button, a text box, and a label?

4.   What property for a label do you set to center a caption automatically? What would the setting be?

At your computer

1.   In an empty form, examine the property BorderStyle. What is its default value?

2.   Change the BorderStyle and run the program. (The program won't do much. To stop it, open the Run menu and choose End.) Try widening the form by dragging an edge. Explain the result of each of the BorderStyle settings.

3.   Create an application that, after the user enters two place names, displays a summary sentence. Be certain to include the period at the end of the sentence. The Start Over button will remove the user's entries and the summary sentence. Figure 2-7 shows the program in action.

Figure 2-7
The Capitals application

Chapter 3   Creating Menus

In this chapter, you learn how to create a pulldown menu and display information based on on the user's menu selection. You also discover how to use **MsgBox**, a Visual Basic command to create a message box, complete with buttons, on the screen. Another helpful built-in Visual Basic feature is **Help**, which is located on the menu bar. As you will see, essential information is always just a few mouse clicks away.

3.1 Creating a pulldown menu

Across the top of many Windows applications is a menu bar. For example, Figure 3-1 shows the Visual Basic 3.0 menu bar with the Run menu pulled down.

Figure 3-1
The Visual Basic 3.0 menu bar

You can easily create similar menu bars for your own applications. The menu system is a set of controls, and each menu choice is a separate control with its own name. To create such a menu, you must open the Menu Design window. To do so, choose the Menu Design option from the Window menu. Before you can enable the Menu Design window, however, the form window must be active. If the Menu Design option is not available from the Window menu, you are probably looking at a code window. Click on the form if you can see it, or click the View Form button on the Project window. (If you can't see the Project window, select it from the Window menu.)

Suppose that you want to create a menu bar such as those shown in Figures 3-2 and 3-3. Along the top of the menu bar are the two main menu choices, File and Edit. Each choice has a submenu that drops down.

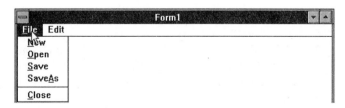

Figure 3-2
A sample menu bar with the File menu pulled down

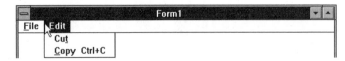

Figure 3-3
A sample menu bar with Edit menu selected

A large application would offer other menu choices. But at this stage in the creation of this particular menu bar, the Menu Design window would look like Figure 3-4. The programmer is in the process of creating the Edit menu's Copy option.

Figure 3-4
A menu bar under construction

First, in the section of the window that shows the list of menu options, note the indentation. To achieve this indentation, you simply click the right arrow button. The indentation of the four dots indicates that Copy is in the Edit menu rather than a top-level choice on the menu bar. (You don't type the four dots; Visual Basic adds them automatically when you click the right arrow button.)

On each line in this section of the window is an individual menu choice, each of which is a control with its own name. The control name that the programmer chose for the Copy option is Copymenu. Try to use a consistent naming convention. To generate a control name, the programmer working on the menu in Figure 3-4 added menu to the caption.

Note that the caption is &Copy. Due to the placement of the ampersand, Visual Basic will underline the *C* in Copy when the option appears in the pulldown menu. The underlining indicates that users can select the Copy option by pressing Alt+C. Similarly, the caption for the **Edit** choice is &Edit. Therefore, the menu bar will display the menu choice as Edit. Copy is an option of the Edit menu, so the underlining indicates that the user can access the Copy option by pressing **Alt+E+C**. If you examine the menu bar in Figure 3-2, you can see the result of the placement of the ampersands in the Save and SaveAs choices.

Other techniques are available. Many applications allow keyboard shortcuts for some menu choices. For example, you can run a Visual Basic program simply by touching F5. In Figure 3-4, the programmer has just assigned the shortcut Ctrl+C to invoke the Edit menu's Copy command. You can assign such shortcuts simply by selecting a suitable hot key in the Shortcut list.

Also in Figure 3-4, notice the line separating the Close option from the rest of the options in the **File** menu. To insert such a line, you enter a hyphen as the caption. You still need a control name such as s1, s2, or s3 for each separating line.

You can also make more deeply nested submenus. Returning to the Menu Design window, how would you produce the modification shown in Figure 3-5?

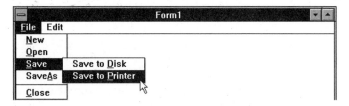

Figure 3-5
Selecting the Save to Printer command from the File menu's Save submenu

To add new menu choices as shown in Figure 3-5, you can press the Insert button in the Menu Design window. Figure 3-6 shows the changes required to add a further submenu under the Save menu choice.

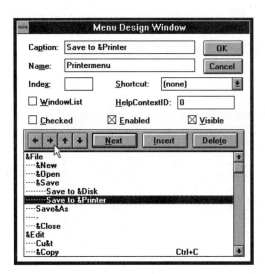

Figure 3-6
Choosing Save brings two more menu choices

3.2 Using the Help screens

Visual Basic provides excellent online information in its Help screens. Figure 3-7 shows Visual Basic's Help menu. By far the most useful option of the Help menu is the Search For Help On choice.

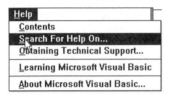

Figure 3-7
Visual Basic's Help menu

For example, an enhancement recommended for applications earlier in this book involved adding a routine to display a message box that that asks, in certain situations, "Are you sure?" You could choose the Search For Help On option to find out details about message boxes.

The Search dialog box, shown in Figure 3-8, contains a combo box and a list box. You can scroll through the combo box or enter a word in the text box at the top. Each letter that you type brings up a topic beginning with your letters. In Figure 3-8, when you begin typing **m**, **e**, and **s**, many topics involving messages fill the combo box. If you select one of these topics, some related subtopics appear in the list box at the bottom of the screen. You can then select any subtopic that seems applicable.

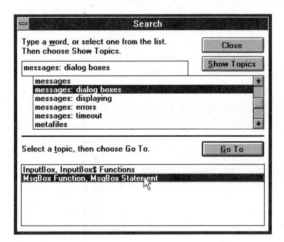

Figure 3-8
Searching for information on message boxes

Many Help topics provide examples that you can study. You can even copy lines from the examples and paste them into your Visual Basic applications. Appendix II shows you how to do this.

The following section explains in more detail what the Help feature tells you about **MsgBox**.

3.3 Using MsgBox: Statements and functions

In Application 1, your code for **Sub** Endbutton consisted of a single statement: **End**. A suggested enhancement provided the following code, which ends the program in a professional way:

```
Sub Endbutton_Click ( )
  if MsgBox("Are you sure?", 36, "Leave Program") = 6 ⇒
    then End
End Sub
```

This code produces on-screen the box shown in Figure 3-9, waits for a button press, and ends the program if the user chooses Yes.

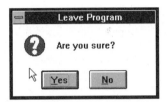

Figure 3-9
An MsgBox example

In the related code, you can see that **MsgBox** has three parameters, or *arguments*. The first is the actual message, which in this case is "Are you sure?" The second is a number that determines which symbols and buttons appear. The last argument is the title of the box.

Now look at Figure 3-10, which shows the Help information on **MsgBox**.

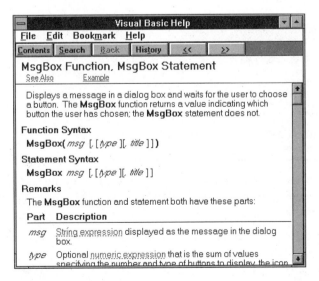

Figure 3-10
Help information on MsgBox

First the information reveals that MsgBox has two uses: as a *function* and as a *statement.*

A statement is an assertion or programming command, such as End or NameBox.Caption = "". In this case, to instruct the computer to display this simple message box, you would use the following MsgBox statement:

```
MsgBox "Save your work first", 16, Exit"
```

The box appears as shown in Figure 3-11 and disappears when the user presses the OK button. As you will soon see, the number 16 codes for a box with stop sign and one OK buttton.

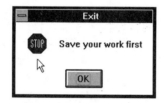

Figure 3-11
A simple message box with an OK button

In everyday speech, "function" means "purpose." But in mathematics and computer programming, a function is a phrase that takes on a value. In the case of MsgBox, the value depends on the user's response.

You would use the MsgBox function to enable your program to check for whether the user pressed a Yes or No button (see Figure 3-12). You could say

```
If MsgBox ("Play Again", 36,"Game Over) = 6 then ...
```

Figure 3-12
A message box that gives the user two choices

Further down on the Help screen you will find the code number that the MsgBox function equals for each button. For example, a 6 indicates that the user pressed Yes.

The Help screen's syntax section shows the actual grammatical use of the expression. The Statement Syntax shows the following:

```
MsgBox msg$ [, type% [, title$ ]]
```

The square brackets indicate optional items; you can disregard them for the moment. Thus the minimum use of the statement, to put a message on the screen in a box with an OK button, is the following:[1]

```
MsgBox msg$
```

An example of this usage is the following:

```
MsgBox "Press OK to Begin", 0,"Project Name"
```

This code results in the message box shown in Figure 3-13.

Figure 3-13
A simple message box

You can use the optional numeric argument to specify the type of box. A box with Yes and No buttons and a large question mark is a type 36 (32 + 4) message box. If you scroll down through the **MsgBox** Help screen and examine the list of numbers for message box types, you see that 32 represents the question mark and 4 represents a box with Yes and No buttons.

Note that you use parentheses (round brackets) in the **MsgBox** function's syntax but not in the statement's syntax.

Application 3   **Making menus and displaying information**

Overview

The Planets application (see Figure 3-14) enables users to receive information about a planet that they select from a pulldown menu.

---

[1] The dollar sign has nothing to do with currency. As you will see in Chapter 4, the entire word that ends in the dollar sign represents a string of characters, such as a letter, word, or sentence.

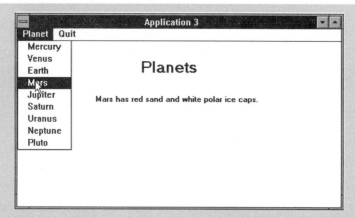

Figure 3-14
The Planets application

Learning objectives

- creating pulldown menus
- creating a message box
- using **Help**

Instructions

You first make a label for the title, with the caption Planets, as shown in Figure 3-15. You can leave its control name as Label1. Open the Properties menu and select FontSize. The font size shown is 18. Center the word in the label. (If you can't remember how to do this, you can simply go to Help and search for the word *Center*.)

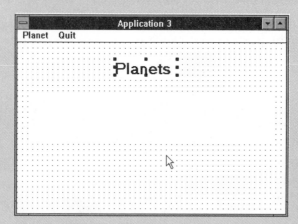

Figure 3-15
The Planets form

Next put a large label box in the center of the form. Make its control name Info and center its caption. Erase its default caption by selecting Caption from the properties list and erasing the phrase Label2.

Open the Window menu and choose Menu Design to display the Menu Design window (see Figure 3-16). In this window, you design the application's complete menu system. Remember that you don't type the dots. To indent a menu option such as Mercury, which makes it a submenu under Planet, press the right arrow key. Press the left-arrow key to start Quit at the margin, so that it appears beside Planet on the finished menu. Choose a unique, meaningful name for each menu option.

Figure 3-16
Creating the menu

After you finish with the last item in the list, click OK. The window closes. Select the form by clicking on it. Then, without starting the program, operate the menu with the mouse. In this way, you can test your new menu. You can also open a code window in which you can add the statements that operate each choice.

Select Mercury and enter the following code:

```
Sub mercurymenu_click ( )
     Info.caption="Mercury is closest to the sun: a ⇒
        hot, dry cratered( planet."
End Sub
```

The **Sub** name contains the name that you chose for the Mercury menu choice. The arrow at the end of the second line indicates that the statement continues on the next line in the book. Don't type the arrow, just continue to type the statement, even if it goes past the edge of your screen display.

Use the following comments for the other planets' entries (or make up your own.):

```
Venus is cloud-covered, with a hot, humid, dense atmosphere.
Earth is the water planet, with a dry, lifeless moon.
```

Mars has red sand and white polar ice caps.
Giant Jupiter is the largest of the planets.
Saturn's famous rings can be seen from earth with a small telescope.
Uranus has several interesting moons.
Neptune is greenish and tipped on its side.
Pluto is tiny and travels in a very elliptical orbit.

Modifications

1. Change the message box to show a stop sign that says "End program." Also, add OK and Cancel buttons and a title that says "Quit." Remember to check for the correct return code.

2. Add to the menu a choice called Astertoids between Mars and Jupiter, as shown in Figure 3-17. In the solar system there is quite a gap between Mars and Jupiter, so include separators before and after the Asteroids menu choice.

Figure 3-17
The Asteroids menu choice with separators

Enhancement

Put a picture on your frame. First add a picture box control from the toolbox. The Picture property shows that the picture box contains no picture (see Figure 3-18). Click on the button with the three dots beside the Settings box above the scroll bar. You can now search your hard drive for icons, pictures, or clip art. Under Visual Basic's \Icons\Elements subdirectory, you should find some icons showing the moon. Also, Word for Windows includes pictures of stars. Elsewhere you might find the signs of the Zodiac. You should be able to find different pictures to display for each menu selection. In the Help screens, search for **loading pictures**.

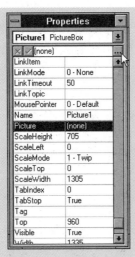

Figure 3-18
The properties list for a new picture box

Exercises

At your desk

1. The toolbar has no control for the menu. How do you bring up the Menu Design window?

2. Use Figure 3-19 to answer the following questions:

a. What does a type 17 message box display?
b. Which number represents a box with stop sign and OK button?

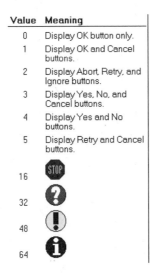

Value	Meaning
0	Display OK button only.
1	Display OK and Cancel buttons.
2	Display Abort, Retry, and Ignore buttons.
3	Display Yes, No, and Cancel buttons.
4	Display Yes and No buttons.
5	Display Retry and Cancel buttons.
16	
32	
48	
64	

Figure 3-19
The MsgBox Help screen

3. What is the difference between a statement and a function?

4. The Help screen for the **Mid$** function[2] shows the following:

Syntax
```
Mid$( stringexpr, start [, length ])
```

a. How many arguments must the **Mid$** function have?
b. Which argument is optional?
c. How many commas are required?
d. You can also use Mid$ as a statement. Of the following valid instructions, which uses Mid$ as a function and which uses it as a statement?

```
Mid$("Hello",2) = "i"
Label1.Caption = Mid$(Label2.Caption,5,2)
```

At your computer

Design an application that enables the user to select from a menu your favorite movies and receive information about them. Figure 3-20 shows such an application. For the display that the application generates, make room for as many as four actors' names, your rating, and some information about the movie (see Figure 3-21). (Of course, you can adapt this application to display plays, books, recipes, or whatever you want.)

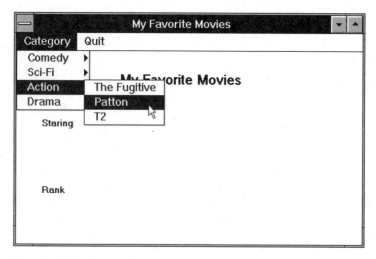

Figure 3-20
The menu-driven My Favorite Movies application

---

[2]To answer these questions, you need not know what the Mid$ function does.

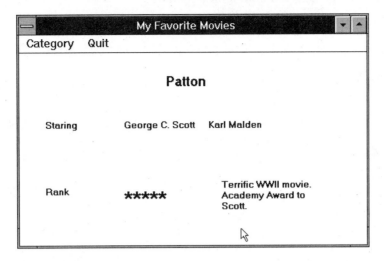

Figure 3-21
A sample display from the My Favorite Movies application

The application should list at least three categories, and each category should present a submenu consisting of at least two choices. Can you find a way to erase the information from the display when the user chooses another category? (Hint: Which action on which control indicates that the user is about to select a new movie? To find that control, check the list of controls in a code window.)

Chapter 4

Using Variables and Making Calculations

This chapter discusses applications that need to perform calculations on data. Such applications must hold the user's data in the computer's memory in a form that enables the program to change the data. For this purpose, you use variables.

4.1 Visual Basic variables

A mathematician calculating the area of a rectangle often thinks in terms of a formula such as the following: area = length × width. If length is 5 and width equals 10, area is 50 (square units). After such a formula is established, the mathematician can calculate the area as long as length and width are specified. The formula could be expressed as

```
A = L * W
```

where the asterisk is a multiplication symbol and L and W are variables–letters that are representing the data.

Variables are letters or words that represent a number, if they are to be used for calculation, or a string of characters. Note the following example:

```
x = 1
```

This expression says that x takes the value 1. In other words, x is a variable whose present value is 1. Therefore, if your application uses a formula that includes +1, it could now also use +x.

You can use any descriptive single word that you want for your variable name, as long as it is not a *reserved word*–a word that Visual Basic itself uses, such as **Caption**, **Sub**, or **End**. To calculate the tax on a $49 purchase, for example, you might choose the following variable names:

```
price = 49
taxrate = .05
tax = price * taxrate    'asterisk is multiplication
```

Another way of understanding the concept of variables is to imagine calling actual memory locations in the computer price, taxrate , and tax. You place values into the locations by stating them explicitly or by calculating them.

Here are some more examples:

```
z = x + y
p = z / 100
perimeter = 2 * (length + width)
count = count + 1           'increases the value of count
```

A mathematician would choke on the last example, because count could never equal count plus one. Remember that the equals sign actually means "takes on the value of." Therefore, the last statement means that count takes on the value of its old value plus one.

Numeric variables

The examples of numeric variables that you have seen hold decimal numbers up to seven digits long. These examples are *single-precision floating-point variables* (or for short, **Single**). By adding the pound sign (#) to the variable name, as in the following example, you can have the computer keep track of twice as many digits:

```
pi# = 3.14159264
```

This is called a *double-precision floating-point variable.* This type of variable is mainly for high-precision calculations; you seldom use it for general calculations.

Another type of variable is the **integer** variable, which holds only whole numbers. If you assign an integer variable a decimal number, the variable stores a rounded-off value. To specify integer variables, you add a percent sign (%) to the variable name, as in the following examples:

```
age% = 45
year% = 1995
a% = 5.8
```

In the last case, **a%** is rounded off to 6.

To store a number greater than 32,767, you need a **long** integer. To specify such an integer, you add an ampersand (&) prefix, as follows:

```
biggest_long_integer& = 2147483647
```

String variables

You can also store letters, words, and other *alphanumeric* characters in a variable. Note the following example:

```
Let firstname$ = "Michelle"
```

firstname$ is a string variable. The dollar sign does not have anything to do with money. When placed at the end of the variable name, a dollar sign specifies that the variable will hold alphanumeric data (strings of characters) rather than numbers for calculating purposes. Think of firstname$ as representing a set (or *string*) of memory locations that contain the letters Michelle.

Here are some other examples:

```
a$ = "Y"
```

```
b$ = "hello"
c$ = "This is a sentence"
d$ = "!@#$%"
e$ = " "          'quote-space-quote          i.e. a space
f$ = ""           'quote quote ..... represents an empty ⇒
   or nil string
address$ = "The address is 123 Main Street"
unit$ = "1"
```

Notice that you use double quotation marks with string variables. The last two examples demonstrate that a string can contain numeric digits. Sometimes a string may contain what looks like a calculation:

```
phone$ = "555-1212"
```

This example is not a subtraction operation. The contents of phone$ will not be −657 (that is, 555–1212). The dollar sign and the quotation marks tell the computer to treat the expression as an eight-letter "word" consisting of characters that happen to look like numeric digits.

Although you can use the plus sign with strings, this use doesn't result in addition. Instead, the character combines the strings into one string, in a process called *concatenation:*[1]

```
a$ = "1" + "2"
```

In this example, a$ becomes 12, not 3.

Suppose that the following four lines are part of a single routine. What will be the contents of name$ and alphaname$?

```
firstname$ = "Pat"
last_name$ = "Buie"
name$ = firstname$ + " " + lastname$
alphaname$ = lastname$ + ", " + firstname$
```

Answer: name$ will be Pat Buie and alphaname$ will be Buie, Pat.

Try the next examples as well. What will be the contents of the numeric variable total and the string variable together$?

```
x = 5 : y = 6 : total = x + y
a$ = "5" : b$ = "6" : together$ = a$ + b$
```

---

[1]Visual Basic now supports *variant* variables, which can shift between being string or numeric variables as the situation requires (or as Visual Basic *thinks* the situation requires). The variable x, for example, can be a numeric variable at one point and later a string variable. Thus the expression x + x could become ambiguous (either addition or concatenation). You can now use the ampersand as a replacement for the plus sign to guarantee concatenation rather than numeric addition. Don't confuse this use of the & operator to concatenate strings (as in msg$ = "hello" & a$) with the operator's use to designate a long integer (as in num& = 2 * y).

Answer: The value of `total` will be `11`, and `together$` will contain the string of characters `56`.

You can define variable names such as `x`, `year`, or `address` as integers or strings. That is, even if the last character of the variable name is not $ or %, the variable could still be a string variable or another defined type of variable. Also, you can define a single variable name to be a mixture of different types.[2]

If you choose to define variables, you will write the definitions in the declarations section of the program. You find this section in the code window under Object: (general) Proc: (declarations). You will not need this technique until Chapter 6.

4.2 Using the contents of text boxes and labels in a calculation

Imagine a simple application in which the user enters the length and width of a rectangle and the computer displays the answer, as shown in Figure 4-1. (As you read this section, you can think through the process of creating the application or actually create it on your computer. The chapter's main application comes later.)

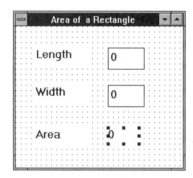

Figure 4-1
The form for calculating a rectangle's area

The application requires two text boxes and four labels. The text boxes, which accept the user's entries, are called LengthBox and WidthBox. The initial text in each box is 0. The answer goes in AreaBox, a label presently showing the caption 0. You use a label rather than a text box because the application, not the user, enters the value.

A text box's text is alphanumeric, as is a label's caption. You can't multiply words. How do you multiply the values together and display the numeric answer as AreaBox's caption, which is also a string? The application needs a way to change strings into numbers so that it can use them in calculations and then change the numbers back to strings so that it can use them in captions.

---

[2]*Variant* variables can change their type, from integer to string to floating point, as the context indicates.

Val and Str$

Two functions, **Val** and **Str$**, serve this purpose. **Val** gets the value of the contents of a string, and **Str$** changes a number to a string. To display the area in your application, you follow these steps:

1.   Change WidthBox.Text and LengthBox.Text to numbers.

2.   Perform the calculations.

3.   Change the answer to a string and store it in AreaBox.Caption.

To convert a word to a number, you use the expression **Val** , as follows:

```
W =   Val(WidthBox.text)
L = Val(LengthBox.text)
```

Then multiply W times L and put the answer in AreaBox.Caption, as follows:

```
AreaBox.Caption = Str$(W * L)
```

Figure 4-2 shows the entire routine put into LengthBox_Change. Now, when the user types a value, the area changes simultaneously. You also place this routine into WidthBox_Change.

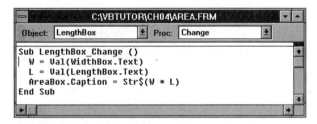

Figure 4-2
The Sub that calculates and places the area in AreaBox

Summary

You've just learned a lot about variables. Here's a quick summary:

A numeric variable holds decimal numbers:

```
x = 1.2
```

An integer numeric variable holds integers:

```
year% = 1995
```

A string variable holds alphanumeric characters:

```
a$ = "My birthday is September 10!"
```

The **Val** of a string is a number:

```
num  =  Val(a$)
```

The **Str$** of a number is a string (text):

```
a$ = Str$(num)
```

You can take the value of a word, but it turns out to be zero. This is sometimes useful, as in the following example:

```
if Val(age.text) = 0 then label1.Caption = "Use numbers
    please"
```

Differences in **Val** and **Str$** use between Visual Basic 3.0 and earlier versions

In early versions of Visual Basic, the following statement generates an error:

```
x = text1.text
```

Visual Basic would assume that you are trying to assign a string to a numeric variable, and thus would send a **Type Mismatch** error.

However, Visual Basic 3.0 has a variable type called **variant**. The preceding statement now makes x a variant variable, unless you previously assigned x be a different type of variable. x then becomes a string variable, even though it does have a dollar sign after it. This feature could result in some confusion and program logic errors. Study the following four lines, which apply to a form that contains three text boxes:

```
x = text1.text
y = text2.text
z = x + y
text3.text = z
```

If text1 holds 1 and text2 holds 2, would the programmer want z to have the value 3 or the string 12? Make up a form that has three text boxes, place the code in text3_click, and then run the program. Click on the third text box and see what the computer assumes.

The answer is that z would be the string variable 11, whereas you might have wanted z to be a numeric variable with value 2. You can see how confusing and dangerous this could be.

Starting with version 3.0 of Visual Basic, you can also omit .Caption or .Text. In other words, Label1 = "hello" is acceptable. The computer assumes that you mean Label1.Caption = "hello". Therefore, you can shorten the previous code to the following:

```
z = label1 + label2
label3 = z
```

In fact, you could even shorten the code to the following:

```
label3 = label1 + label2
```

Visual Basic 3.0 forgives errors of omission. Therefore, it takes x = text1 to mean x$ = text1 text. Visual Basic's programmers were kind to build in this mind-reading capability. Nevertheless, this book always uses the longer, more precise wordings to prevent unanticipated logical errors, as in the following examples:

```
x$ = text1.text
x = Val(text1.text)
text1.text = "hello"
```

Application 4   Sales tax

Overview

With the Sales Tax application (see Figure 4-3), the user enters the sales tax percent and the amount of the purchases. When the user presses the Calculate button, the computer calculates the tax and the total.

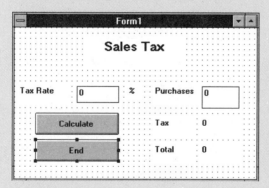

Figure 4-3
The Sales Tax form during the design stage

Learning objectives

- using **Val** to store the contents of a text box in a variable
- calculating with variables
- using text boxes, labels, and command buttons
- displaying numbers in text boxes

Instructions

The form includes eight labels and two text boxes. Make a label for the title and then labels for the four words. Another tiny label has % as its caption. The user enters two values: the tax rate and the dollar value of the purchases. For these values, create two text boxes called TaxRateBox and PurchasesBox.

The application will fill in the dollar values for the tax and total, so make two labels called TaxBox and TotalBox. (Don't use text boxes, because you don't want the user to enter anything for these values. Instead, the application will automatically enter them.)

Make the two buttons, End and Calculate. EndButton has the usual code, but CalcButton contains the important routine:

```
Sub CalcButton_Click ()
   taxrate = Val(TaxRateBox.Text)        'convert text in the boxes ...
   purchases = Val(PurchasesBox.Text)    ' to numbers
   tax = purchases * taxrate / 100       'calculate the tax
   total = purchases + tax               'add tax to total
   TaxBox.Caption = str$(tax)            'make the numbers into ...
   TotalBox.Caption = str$(total)        '..strings and ⇒
                                         display answers
End Sub
```

Modifications

1. Currently, the user has to press the Calculate button to recalculate the answers after changing the tax rate. To make the application more convenient, put the CalcButton_Click code into TaxRateBox_Change. The quickest way is to use the Edit menu's Copy and Paste commands. Highlight the CalcButton_Click routine and choose Copy from the Edit menu. Then double-click on TaxRateBox or bring up its TaxRateBox_Click window by selecting from the Object pulldown list. Click below the Sub TaxRateBox_Change() line and choose Paste from the Edit menu. Make sure that you don't end up with two End Sub lines.

2. What else would you have to do to make the application work without any Calculate button?

3. The form shows purchase price, tax, and total price. Make the form more flexible so that it enables the user to make a partial payment. Modify your form to show Deposit and Balance Owed rather than Total.

Enhancements

When you run the program, you will notice that it sometimes doesn't display dollars and cents values correctly. Set the tax rate at 5 and the purchases to 110. You would rather have the answer show 115.50. Visual Basic enables you to do this by supplying the **Format$** function. Like **Str$**, Format$ turns values into strings. However, Format$ also enables you to specify the number of digits before and after the decimal.

Change the lines with Str$ to the following:

```
TaxBox.Caption = Format$(tax, "######.00")
TotalBox.Caption = Format$(total, "######.00")
```

"#####.00" is the pattern that the application is to display. The pound signs tell the computer to display a nonzero digit if necessary. The zeros tell the computer to display a digit even if it is zero. Search for Format$ in the Help screens for other features.

Exercises

At your desk

1. State the type of variable that each of the following represents (assuming that they were not previously defined as something else):

   a.   num
   b.   num%
   c.   num$

2. If x = 2, y = 1.6, and z = 1, state the value of z in each of the following cases:

   a.   z = z + 1
   b.   z = x + 1
   c.   z = x * y
   d.   z = (x + y) / 2

3. If a$ = "SUN", b$ = "DAY", c$ = "1", and d$ = "2", state the contents of e$ in each of the following cases:

   a.   e$ = a$ + b$
   b.   e$ = c$ + d$
   c.   e$ = a$ + "NY "+ b$
   d.   e$ = ""   '(quote-quote)

4. If a$ = "2" and b$ = "3", state the contents of x% in each of the following cases:

   a.   x% = Val(a$ + b$)
   b.   x% = Val(a$) + Val(b$)
   c.   x% = Val(a$ + b$) / 3

5. What is wrong with each of the following?

   a.   x% = Label1.Caption
   b.   a$ = Str$(Text1.text)
   c.   a$ = Val(Command1.Caption)
   d.   x% = 40000

At your computer

1. Create the form shown in Figure 4-4. When the user wants to convert the temperature from Fahrenheit to Celsius, he or she clicks the = button. The equivalent Celsius temperature then appears in the Celsius window.

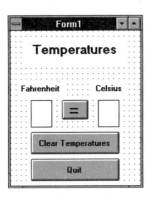 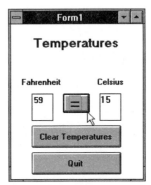

Figure 4-4
The Temperatures form

The formula is as follows:

Celsius temperature = (Fahrenheit temperature − 32) * 5 / 9

2. Create the Calculations form shown in Figure 4-5. The form consists of two text boxes, six labels, and four buttons.

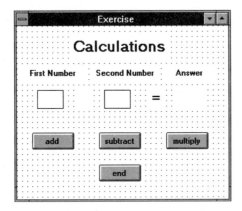

Figure 4-5
The Calculations form during the design stage

When the user clicks one of the three arithmetic buttons, a plus, minus, or times sign appears between the two numbers, and the correct answer appears in the text box after the equals sign.

Figure 4-6 shows the running program after the user enters the numbers **4** and **6** and then presses the **add** button.

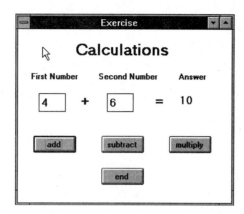

Figure 4-6
The running Calculations form

Chapter 5 aking Decisions

Few computer programs run by themselves, without the user's interaction. An example of a program that runs by itself is one that displays a "ticking" clock on-screen. But the most interesting programs are those that behave differently depending on user input or the results of calculations.

For example, an application that calculates how much a stock purchase will cost depending on the price and number of shares might be useful. But suppose that you have a stock management program that, when fed rules, prices, and your strategies, goals, and investment portfolio, could advise you when to buy or sell.[1] Such a program would need to be much more flexible if it were to respond in many different ways depending on your input.

To write flexible programs that are more complex than you have created so far, you use two basic types of structures: the *If ... Then ... Else* structure and *Select Case*.

5.1 Deciding between two alternatives

In this chapter's application, the user enters school grades into text boxes. The computer decides whether the mark is over or under 50 percent and judges whether it is a passing or failing grade.

The If ... Then Structure

To write such an application, a single-line **If ... Then** statement is appropriate:

```
If mark >= 50 Then credits = credits + 1
```

This statement says that if the number represented by the variable mark is greater than or equal to 50, increase credits by one. The instruction after **Then** executes only if the condition is true; otherwise, the program continues with the subsequent instruction.

---

[1]Programs are available that provide such financial advice. Some will actually, without your guidance, make a telephone connection to a stock prices provider and download the data relevant to your portfolio. The program then maintains the values in data files on your drive. The next time that you run the program, it is ready to advise you. Don't confuse these programs with the "programmed trading" that some analysts have considered responsible for large fluctuations in the stock market. Those application programs don't just advise when to sell, but also make the transaction all on their own. Such applications are examples of some very sophisicated (and, perhaps, dangerous) decision-making indeed.

The If ... Then ... Else Structure

Suppose that you also want to count failures. In such a case, you can use a single-line **If ... Then ... Else** statement:

```
If mark >= 50 Then credits = credits + 1 Else failures ⇒
    = failures + 1
```

A single-line **If** statement has the following form:

```
If this statement is true, Then do this Else do ⇒
    something else
```

The condition and the two alternatives can be any valid statements, as in the following examples:

```
x = 10
y > 0
a$ = ""
AddressBox.Text = "123 Main Street"
```

Therefore, the following could be a valid **If ... Then ... Else** statement:

```
If x=10 Then a$ = "" Else AddressBox.Text = "123 Main ⇒
    Street"
```

The If ... End If Structure

Sometimes you want your program to perform different actions depending on whether a condition is true or false. To do so, you use the **If ... End If** structure.

In Figures 5-1 and 5-2, notice that the prompt changes when the user starts typing a name. Also note that the OK button is disabled (inoperative) until the user starts typing. Therefore, when the user enters a name, the program must do two things: change the caption of the prompt (InstructionBox) and enable the OK button.

Figure 5-1
Before the user enters a name

Figure 5-2
As the user is entering a name

Here is the code that performs these actions:

```
If NameBox.Text = "" Then        'if there is nothing in ⇒
     NameBox
   InstructionBox.Caption = "Please enter your name"
   OKbutton.enabled = False      'deactivate the OK button
Else
   InstructionBox.Caption = "Please press the OK button"
   OKbutton.enabled = True       'activate the OK button
End If
```

The following is the general structure for an **If ... End If** block:

```
If this statement is true Then
   Do something
   Do this also
Else
   Do that
End If
```

The first line of the multiline **If** structure must end with **Then**. But the computer will not know which of the subsequent lines ends the structure unless you insert the **End If**.

Note also that the structure does not require an **Else**:

```
If this statement is true Then
   Do this
   Do this also
   And do that
End If
```

If the statement is false, the computer just moves on to whatever follows the **End If** statement, having done nothing.

5.2 Choosing from several alternatives: Select Case

In this section, you develop a simple application that makes many choices. The form is similar to that in Figures 5-1 and 5-2, in which the user enters a name and the prompt changes. However, in this application, the user enters his or her age and the computer makes a comment. Figure 5-3 shows the application generating comments for several different responses.

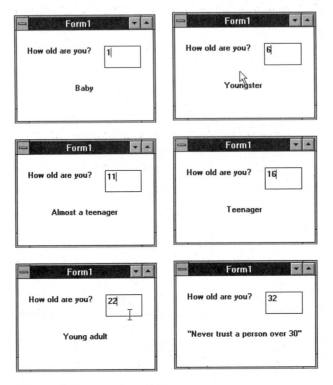

Figure 5-3
The form's comment depends on the value that the user enters in the text box.

Suppose that Comment.Caption controls the caption and AgeBox.Text accepts the value that the user enters in the text box. You could code the choices for Comment.Caption by using many **If** statements:

```
age = Val(AgeBox.Text)
If age <= 2 Then Comment.Caption = "Baby"
If age > 2 And age <= 3 Then Comment.Caption = ⇒
  "Toddler"
If age > 3 And age <=11 Then Comment.Caption = ⇒
  "Youngster"
If age > 11 And age < 13 Then Comment.Caption = ⇒
  "Almost a teenager"
... and so on
```

This method is cumbersome and slow. A better method uses the **Select Case** statement:

```
Select Case Val(AgeBox)
  Case Is <= 1
    comment = "Baby"
```

```
   Case 1 To 3
     comment = "Toddler"
   Case 3 To 10
     comment = "Youngster"
   Case 11 To 12
     comment = "Almost a teenager"
   Case 13 To 19
     comment = "Teenager"
   Case 19 To 30
     comment = "Young adult"
   Case Else
     comment = Chr$(34) + "Never trust a person over 30" ⇒
       + Chr$(34)
     'Chr$(34) is Quotes. By adding a Chr$(34) to the ⇒
       beginning
     'and the end of comment, you can display the quotes.
   End Select
```

(In Visual Basic 1.0, you would have had to say Comment.Caption = "such and such" rather than comment = "such and such". However, Visual Basic 3 "reads your mind" and correctly anticipates what you meant even though you omitted .Caption.)

Case Else is a useful feature that enables you to ensure that the user doesn't enter anything that doesn't qualify as a valid response. Always use **Case Else**, even if you don't put any code after it:

```
   Select Case a$
     Case "Y"
       x = -1
       y = 5
     Case "N"
       x = 0
       y = 0
     Case Else
   End Select
```

In the preceding example, if the user's entry is other than Y or N, the program performs no conversion to x or y; instead, the program simply moves on to the next line. Notice that you can have more than one statement in each **Case**.

Select Case works with strings as well as numbers, as the following portions of some **Select Case** blocks demonstrate:

```
   Select Case day.Text
     Case Monday
       Greeting = "Start of the Week"
     Case Friday
       Greeting = "Hurrah for Friday"
     and so on ...
   End Select
```

```
Select Case Ucase$(letterbox.Text)
  Case "A", "E", "I", "O", "U"
    message.Text = "It's a vowel"
  Case Else
    message.Text = "It's a consonant"
End Select
```

The last example demonstrates the use of a useful Visual Basic function, **Ucase$**. If you compare something to **Ucase$** *(any string)*, the string can consist of upper- or lowercase characters, or a mixture. However, the comparison string must contain all uppercase letters. For example, the following code works regardless of whether the user enters a$ in upper- or lowercase:

```
If Ucase$(a$) = "Y" Then
      user meant yes
Else
      user meant no
End if
```

5.3 Disabling and enabling controls: the Enabled property

In the code for the form in Section 5.1, did you understand how the programmer enabled and disabled the OK button? You will find Enabled on the properties list for buttons (and other controls). By default, Visual Basic sets Enabled to **True**. For the example form, the programmer set OKbutton.enabled to **False** when designing the form. The computer translates the **False** setting to the value 0. The **True** setting, on the other hand, is equivalent to −1.[2]

5.4 The Change event

You may have noticed that the form shown in Figure 5.3 has no Begin button. What, then, triggers the words that appear in the comment area? The programmer could have added a Begin or Continue button to trigger this event, but did not. Instead, the comments change as the user types. For example, typing 1 for the age brought up "Baby," but if the user then typed 8, the comment changed to "Teenager" (for 18).

How do you enable the program to do this? Remember the object-oriented, event-driven (OO/ED) programming languages[3] rule: Ask yourself which user action is to trigger the appearance of the comment. If you decide that the action should be for the user to press a Comment button, then you create such a button and put the code in that button's Click routine. But you can also display the comment as the user changes the value (by typing or backspacing) in AgeBox. To do so, you place the **Select Case** code into **Sub** Agebox_Change.

---

[2]In earlier versions of Visual Basic, True and False were not reserved words; they did not, in themselves, have value in the code unless you first defined them globally as −1 and 0 respectively. But in Visual Basic 3.0, True and False are reserved words with built-in values.

[3]Object Oriented/Event Driven

Application 5 The Report Card

Overview

The user enters the marks for four subjects. The computer counts the number of failures, computes an average, and provides a letter grade and comment.

Learning objectives

- using **Select Case**
- using general **Sub** procedures
- counting
- calculating
- enabling controls
- indenting code lines

Instructions

Create the form

Figure 5-4 shows the form at design time and during a sample run. Starting at the left side of the form, make all the labels, including the title and the central label at the bottom. Call this bottom label Comment. Moving down the right side of the form, make four text boxes. Change all their text to 0 and make their names MusicBox, MathematicsBox, ScienceBox, and HistoryBox. Next on the left side are three labels that contain the captions Average, Grade, and Failures. Beside each are labels, each with caption 0, called AverageBox, GradeBox, and FailuresBox. At bottom is the familiar End button.

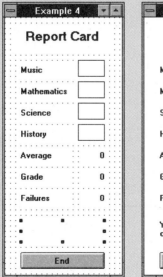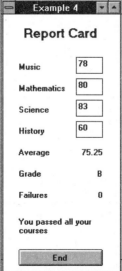

Figure 5.4
The Report Card form, during and after design time

Here is what you want the program to do when the user runs it. First, the user begins typing his or her grades. The form has no Calculate button, so the program should perform calculations when any value in a text box changes. Instead of having the average appear before the user enters all marks, have the program display the average, grade, failures, and comments only after values are in all four text boxes.

To calculate the statistics when any change occurs in the value of a mark in a text box, the events for which you code are MusicBox_Change, MathematicsBox_Change, ScienceBox_Change, and HistoryBox_Change.

You could write the same code in each of the four Change events. However, a faster method is to enter the code under **Sub** *MusicBox_Change and then use the Edit menu's Copy and Paste commands to copy the code in the other three text boxes' Change* **Sub** *procedures. But a better way is to write the code once, store it in a general (nonevent)* **Sub**, *and have the Change events all call (refer to) that* **Sub**.

Display a code window by double-clicking any control. Then, at the top or bottom of an **End Sub** statement, type **Sub Calc**. The computer then sets up a new **Sub** procedure called Calc, which is not linked to any code. Here is the entire Calc routine (explanations follow):

```
Sub Calc ()
  ' **** store the marks in variables mu, ma, sc, and ⇒
    hi
  mu = Val(MusicBox.Text)
  ma = Val(MathematicsBox.Text)
  sc = Val(ScienceBox.Text)
  hi = Val(HistoryBox.Text)
  ' **** see if there are entries in each box (See ⇒
    note below)
  If MusicBox <> "" And MathematicsBox <> "" And ⇒
    ScienceBox <> "" And ⇒HistoryBox <> "" Then ⇒
    ' means continue at end of previous line

    average = (mu + ma + sc + hi) / 4      'calculate ⇒
      average
    AverageBox.Caption = Str$(average)       'place ⇒
      it in the box
  '**** assign the grade letter to GradeBox.Caption
    Select Case average
      Case Is >= 90
      GradeBox.Caption = "A+"
      Case 80 To 90
      GradeBox.Caption = "A"
      Case 70 To 80
      GradeBox.Caption = "B"
      Case 60 To 70
      GradeBox.Caption = "C"
      Case 50 To 60
```

```
              GradeBox.Caption = "D"
           Case Else
              GradeBox.Caption = "E"
        End Select

   ' **** count failures
        fail = 0      'first set fail to 0 in case it had a ⇒
           previous value
        If mu < 50 Then fail = fail + 1        'increase fail
        If ma < 50 Then fail = fail + 1
        If sc < 50 Then fail = fail + 1
        If hi < 50 Then fail = fail + 1
        FailuresBox = fail
        'in VB 1.0, above line would be FailuresBox.Caption ⇒
           = Str$(fail)

   ' **** put suitable message in Comment.Caption
        If fail = 0 Then
           Comment.Caption = "You passed all your courses"
        Else
           Comment.Caption = "You failed " + Str$(fail) + ⇒
              "courses."
        End If
     End If
  End Sub
```

Visual Basic 3.0 is very forgiving. For the preceding code lines that begin Comment.Caption =, you could omit .Caption. The same trick is used to shorten the long **If** statement, which you could begin as follows:

```
   If MusicBox.Text <> "" and ...
```

There is no control called Calc. If you pull down the list of objects, you see all your labels and text boxes, but no Calc control (see Figure 5.5). At the top of the list, you see the choice **(general)**. If you select that object, you see in the Proc box the word **(declarations)**. Pull down the Proc list and you should see your Calc routine.

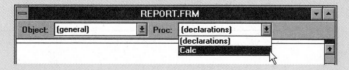

Figure 5.5
Find general Subs below (declarations)

Now go to each of the subject text boxes and have each one call Calc. You don't have to go back to the form and double-click on each text box; just stay in the code window and select the text boxes from the Object list one by one. You make HistoryBox's Change routine look like this:

```
Sub HistoryBox_Change ()
   Calc
End Sub
```

Repeat these changes for MathematicsBox, MusicBox, and ScienceBox.

Now all you need to do is code your End button. If you haven't yet done so, change the form caption and format the title.

Take some time to note the following fine points of coding that the Calc routine demonstrates.

Indentation

The Calc routine is pretty long, with **If** statements within **If** statements. You can easily forget an **End If** or an **End Select**. If you do so, the error messages that Visual Basic displays at run time are sometimes misleading, as it tries to figure out what you intended it to do. Use indentation to keep track of your blocks of associated code.

Every time that you begin a new **If ... End If**, indent the contained lines. In the following example, each indentation is one tab (two spaces in this example):

```
If x = 1 Then
  do statement 1      'indent one Tab
  If x = y Then z = 0 'completed If statement. Don't ⇒
    indent after it.
  If y = 0 Then
    do statement 2 'indent again because it's a second ⇒
      If ... End If
    do statement 3
  Else             'back one Tab
    do statement 4
    Select Case z
      Case first case 'in one Tab
        do statement 5   'in another Tab
      Case else
        do statement 6
    End Select          'go back two Tabs for an End
    Select
    do statement 7
  End If
Else
  do statement 8
End If
```

Indenting helps you see the code's overall logic—which statements the program executes under which circumstances. Also, as you write the code, if you reach the bottom and are not back to the left margin, you know that you have omitted a statement. Finally, in a long list of statements that is longer than one screen, you can find which **If** statement applies to a certain **End If** by putting your cursor on the E of **End If** and moving up the screen quickly with the up-cursor arrow key. The first I that you find should be that of the **If** that starts that block of code.

The order of cases in the Select Case statement.

Consider the order of cases in the ranges in **Sub** Calc's **Select Case** statement. First you checked to see if the average was greater than or equal to 90, then if it was between 80 and 90, then 70 to 80, and so on. If you did not specify these cases in thisthe opposite order, a 90 would get an A, not an A+. To understand why, study **Sub** Calc. (A question in the exercises deals with this issue.)

A quick way to test for nonzero marks in each box.

If you would never give a student a zero, you could shorten the very long line that checks for entries in every box to the following:

```
If mu * ma * sc * hi <> 0 Then
```

Modifications

1. When you run your application, you may notice a grammatical error when only one mark is less than 50 percent. Fix the error. (Hint: Use an **If** statement that checks for the value of fail.)

2. Before running the program, set the Enabled property for Endbutton to **False**. Enable the button only when all four text boxes are filled in. You will have to decide where to put this line:

```
Endbutton.Enabled = True
```

Start entering marks and see whether the button becomes enabled as the comment appears. What happens if you erase one mark? Does the program disable the End button again? Where should you make Enabled **False**?

3. Add a Clear button that erases all entries so that you can start again. This button should disable the End button.

Enhancements

1. Enable the user to enter the subject names. In addition to checking that all marks are entered, the program should not do the calculations until the user has entered the names.

2. Modify the comment or add other comment boxes that state (by name) which subjects the student has failed.

Exercises

At your desk

1. What is the value of xxx after the following code is executed?

```
a = 0 : xxx = 0
If a = 0 Then xxx = 5 Else xxx = 6
```

2. What is the value of xxx after the following code is executed?

```
a = 0 : xxx = 0
If a > 0 Then xxx = 10
```

3. Study this Select Case routine:

```
Select Case t
  Case Is < 5
  Case Is = 5
    xxx = 1
  Case 5 To 10
    xxx = 2
  Case 11 To 20
    xxx = 3
  Case Else
End Select
```

What is the value of xxx after this code is executed when

a. t = 0
b. t = 5
c. t = 10
d. t = 10.5
e. t = 11
f. t = 21

4. Find the error in the following routine:

```
Sub Routine1
  If text1.Text <> "Hello" Then
    label1.Caption = "Ready"
End Sub
```

5. Find the error in the following routine:

```
Sub Endbutton_Click
  If text1.Text = "Good-bye"
  Then End
  End If
End Sub
```

6. Show that these two algorithms produce the same result, assuming that the value of switch is either −1 or 0 before entering the routine.

a. `switch = -1 - switch`
b. `If switch = True Then switch = False Else switch = True`

At your computer

1. Create a form with two text boxes, one for Males and one for Females. Depending on the values in each box, a comment line should say "There are more males than females" or "There are more females than males" or "There is the same number of males and females." (Bonus: Indicate how many more females or males there are, as in "There are two more males than females." Bonus Bonus: Correct the comment line's grammar if there is one more male or female.)

2. In Application 3, **Planets**, the user picked a planet from a menu. Create a form that has a text box, planet.box, instead of the menu. The user simply enters the name of the planet. Use a **Select Case** routine to compare the contents of planet.box to the planet names. Review the last examples in Section 5.2 to see how to make a successful match regardless of whether the user entered the names in upper- or lowercase.

If you saved the Planets program, you can copy the text and paste it into a simple text editor, such as Write. Keep both Visual Basic and your Planets application open but on different sides of the screen. Select each passage and then copy and paste it into Write. After capturing all the planet text, start the new application (the one that you are creating) and copy the whole application into whichever control event you want to use. Modify the application to be a **Select Case** routine.

Chapter 6

☐ ☐ ☐

Using Scroll Bars and Color, and Passing Variables between Subs

Color attracts the user's attention to important information or controls on your form. Scroll bars enable the user to enter values without using the keyboard. In this chapter, you see how to use both color and scroll bars in your programs. You also learn how to pass values of variables between **Subs**. Did you wonder why there are parentheses in Sub Endbutton_Click ( )?

6.1 Adding Color

To add color to your application, four methods are available: the color palette, the long color numbers and hexidecimal notation, the QBColor( ) function, and the RGB( ) function.

Choosing color from the color palette

If you want to add color to your form at design time, open the color palette window. To do so, simply choose Color Palette from the Window menu, as shown in Figure 6-1.

Figure 6-1
Selecting Color Palette

The color palette, shown in Figure 6-2, provides a set of built-in shades and colors from which you can choose. You can color your form, any controls, and text.

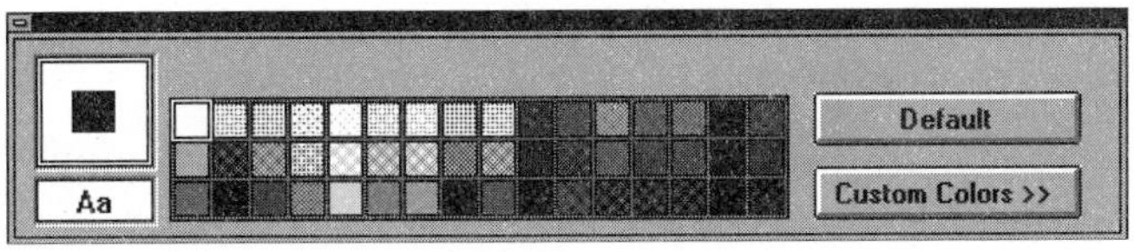

Figure 6-2
The color palette

The relevant controls are BackColor and ForeColor. BackColor is the color of the label itself, while ForeColor is the text color. To use the color palette to set these controls, first select the control (such as the text box, form, or label) that you want to color. Then click in the center black square on the left side of the color palette window. Then click on a color to set your ForeColor, which is the text's color. To choose a background color, click in the box outside the center square and then click on a color displayed in the palette.

Some text colors don't display well against some backgrounds. The box in the lower left enables you to preview your selection. Text looks best when you choose a solid BackColor and ForeColor.

You can select your colors from a palette without opening the color palette itself.

The ellipsis (...) button of the Properties window opens a miniature palette. In Figure 6-3, the user is about to click this button.

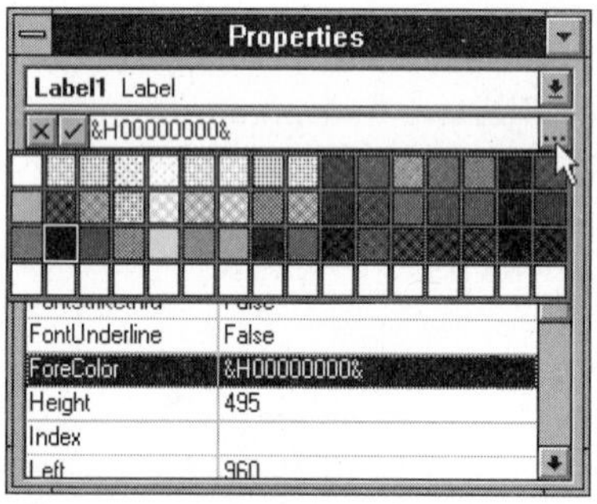

Figure 6-3
Setting colors from the Properties window

The long color numbers and hex notation

In Figure 6-3, notice that the Properties window displays the following as the actual description of the color in the properties box:

&H80000008&

This is the number that Visual Basic uses to identify the color. The &H indicates that the number is in *hex* notation (hexadecimal, or base 16). You could type a number such as 1234567 in decimal, and the text would change to a shade of green; however, Visual Basic would convert the number to base 16 and display the number in hex notation. *You need not know how to do this to use color effectively.*

Using QBColor( )

Visual Basic's coding language derives from QuickBASIC, the advanced form of QBasic that comes with DOS 5 and 6. In that non-Windows language, the programmer could use any of the 16 colors listed in Table 6.1.

Table 6.1　QBasic color numbers

Color Number	Color	Color Number	Color
0	Black	8	Gray
1	Blue	9	Bright blue
2	Green	10	Bright green
3	Cyan	11	Bright cyan
4	Red	12	Bright red
5	Violet	13	Bright violet
6	Orange	14	Yellow
7	White	15	Bright white

Although the 16 colors in Table 6-1 present a limited choice, an easy way to color a control is to use the **QBColor**( ) function. Simply enter one of the listed numbers within the function's parentheses. The following code makes the ForeColor of the control named Stoplight either red or green:

```
Sub ChangeTextColor
   If Stoplight.Caption = "GO" then
     Stoplight.ForeColor = QBColor(2)
   Else
     Stoplignt.ForeColor = QBColor(4)
   End If
```

Using the RGB( ) function

Another way to control color is to use three numbers between 0 and 255 to set the amounts of red, green, and blue respectively. Application 6, later in this chapter, shows you how to do this.

6.2　Passing variable values between procedures

Application 6 changes background and foreground colors. To select a color number, the user uses a scroll bar. Your program has to pass this value between various **Subs**. There are some important facts that you must know about this process.

Variables are, by default, local to the **Sub** in which they appear

If you use the same variable in two different **Subs**, the value of the variable in one **Sub** does not affect the variable's value in the other **Sub**. For example, suppose that you are working on the form shown in Figure 6-4.

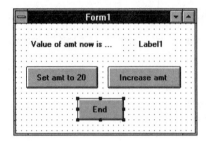

Figure 6-4
Testing variable values

The following is the code for the Set amt to 20 button:

```
Sub SetButton_Click ()
  amt = 20
  Label1.Caption = Str$(amt)
End Sub
```

The Increase amt button has this code:

```
Sub IncreaseButton_Click ()
  amt = amt + 1
  Label1.Caption = Str$(amt)
End Sub
```

When you press the Set amt to 20 button, Label1's caption becomes 20. Pressing the right button makes Label1's caption 1, not 21. Therefore, even though **Sub** SetButton_Click previously set amt to 20, in **Sub** IncreaseButton_Click, amt begins with the value zero. The value of a variable is *local* to the **Sub** in which it appears.

Values of variables are cleared at the beginning of a Sub

Unless you write a statement to the contrary, the value of all variables used in the **Sub** begins at zero each time that the program enters the **Sub**. In the preceding example, repeatedly pressing the Increase amt button does not make amt go higher than one.

You can allow the variable to maintain its value in the Sub

If you want the **Sub** to remember the value of its variables from the last time that the program called the **Sub**, you can add a **Static** statement:

```
Sub IncreaseButton_Click ()
  Static amt as integer    'define amt as an integer ⇒
```

```
      whose value holds
   amt = amt + 1 'increase amt from its current value in ⇒
      the Sub
   Label1.caption =  amt
End Sub
```

This code shows `amt` defined as a **Static** integer. If you enter **Sub** IncreaseButton_Click a second time (by pressing the Increase amt button twice), the label displays a 2. As before, changes to `amt` in other **Subs** do not affect `amt`'s value, so `amt` is still a local variable.

All Subs know the value of a global variable

Suppose that you want all subprocedures to know the variable `amt`. For example, after pressing the Set amt to 20 button, you want IncreaseButton to make the value 21. IncreaseButton would have to know the value of `amt` outside of the **Sub**, and not set it to zero inside of **Sub** IncreaseButton_Click. In other words, you would have to make the value *global.*

In the code window, select (general) from the Object list and (declarations) from the Proc list. Enter this line:

```
Dim amt as Integer
```

Remove the **Static** line from **Sub IncreaseButton_Click** and add the following line to Form_Load:

```
Sub Form_Load
   amt = 100
End Sub
```

When you run the program and press the Increase amt button, `amt` takes on the value 101 (after being increased by the `amt = amt + 1` statement). Pressing the Set amt to 20 button followed by the Increase amt button makes `amt` equal to 21. The dimension line (the line that begins with **Dim**) makes the variable `amt` global to all procedures for all controls on that form. In other words, all those controls know the current value of `amt`, and the program does not set `amt` to zero upon exiting any form.

You can pass a specific value to a variable in a Sub

If you create your own subprocedure, you can include one or more variables in parentheses after the name that you chose for the **Sub**. These variables will not be automatically set at zero or resume their previous value when the program enters the **Sub**. Instead, they take on the value that you state in the instruction that calls the **Sub**.

For example, note the following **Sub** called ShowIt:

```
Sub ShowIt (a)
  Label1.Caption = Str$(a)    'place variable a in the ⇒
    label
  a = a + 1                   'increase a by one
End Sub
```

Any other **Sub** can invoke ShowIt simply by mentioning its name followed by a number or numeric variable (*not necessarily the variable* a). Each of the following three example Subs handle the clicking of a button on the form, call ShowIt, pass it the value 2, and cause a 2 to appear in Label1:

```
Sub Command1_Click ()
  ShowIt 2    'call ShowIt and pass a 2
End Sub

Sub Command1_Click ()
  x = 2
  ShowIt x 'call ShowIt and pass the value of x
End Sub

Sub Command1_Click ()
  x = 1
  ShowIt x+1   'call ShowIt and pass the value of x
End Sub
```

The ShowIt routine includes a line that increases the variable a by one. This code line causes the value of variable x to change in the last two of the preceding routines. When two **Subs** pass the values of variables, the passing goes both ways: a takes on x's value, a gets changed, and x takes on a's new value. The variable names need not be the same. All that matters is that if more than one variable is in the list, the program sends the variables in the correct order. For example, suppose that you had the following **Sub**:

```
Sub Greeting (a$, a)
  Label1.Caption = "Congratulations " + a$ +" for ⇒
    becoming "+Str$(a) " years old"
End Sub
```

You could call this **Sub** with either of the following lines:

```
Greeting Robert, 25

Greeting name$, age
```

However, you could not call the **Sub** with the following:

```
Greeting 25, Robert
```

Application 6 Using scroll bars to set color

Overview

By sliding this application's scroll bars, the user can change the colors of controls on the form.

Learning objectives

- making a scroll bar
- using option buttons
- setting conditions at run time
- using **RGB( )**, a built-in Visual Basic color function
- passing variables between Subs

Instructions

Select a horizontal scroll bar from the Toolbox and place it on the form as shown in Figure 6-5. Change the scroll bar's name to RedBar. Place a label to its left with both name and caption as Red, and a label to the right with the name redvalue and the caption 0 (zero). Call the top label Title and use a larger font for the centered caption.

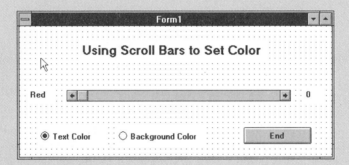

Figure 6-5
The form at design time

After placing a scroll bar on the form, you must set its maximum and minimum values. Min and Max are the appropriate properties to set.

At run time, when the form loads, you can also set the scroll bar's limits. To do so, double-click on the form itself (not on one of the controls). This displays the form's code window. Select Load from the form's action (Proc) list. Then enter the following code:

```
Sub Form_Load ()
   RedBar.min = 0
   RedBar.max = 255
End Sub
```

The user will use the scroll bar to set the amount of red in the title's BackColor or ForeColor. To make this work, you use Visual Basic's red-green-blue function, with the following syntax:

```
RGB(number1, number2, number3)
```

The RGB( ) function has three arguments: the amounts of red, green, and blue that make up the color. The range of numbers is 0 to 255, which is why RedBar.Max is set to 255. Double-click on the scroll bar and enter this code:

```
Sub RedBar_Change ()
    title.BackColor = RGB(RedBar.Value, 0, 0)
End Sub
```

As the preceding code indicates, you read the scroll bar by examining its Value property. If you need the property for calculation purposes, you can store it in a variable:

```
bc = RedBar.Value
```

Usually scroll bars start at zero, but you can set its value to any number between Min and Max.

```
'in Form_Load ...
RedBar.Value = initialvalue 'whatever starting number ⇒
    you wish
```

After you create and code the End button, run the program. (You'll add the option buttons in a moment.) If everything is working properly so far, the scroll bar should change the title's background from black to red.

Now you can add the two option buttons, TextC and BackC. If the user selects the Text Color option, the scroll bar will determine Title.ForeColor. If the Background Color option is chosen, the scroll bar will set Title.BackColor. Thus the option buttons work as a team. Only one can be on (**True**) at a time. When you turn on one of the options, the other button turns off (**False**).

Because the program uses the scroll bar to determine two different properties, you must use variables. The `fc` variable stands for the scroll bar setting when the scroll bar is controlling title's ForeColor. The variable `bk` stands for the scroll bar setting for the BackColor.[1]

When the program begins, BackColor will be red, which requires `bk` to be 255 (the maximum setting on the scroll bar). The text is black, so `fc` is zero. You can make the scroll bar initially control the background text color. Therefore, the Text Color option button should be **False** and the Background Color button **True**. You

---

[1] Note that the variables stand for the scroll bar setting (between 0 and 255), not the color number itself, which is RGB(scroll bar value, 0, 0).

can set these at design time, but it is handy to set them at run time, at the same time that you set the scroll bar's minimum and maximum values. Put the necessary instructions in Form_Load, which is executed as the program starts.[2] Thus in Form_Load you must set the values of the variables, the corresponding colors, and the option buttons, and make the scroll bar display the background reading of 0:

```
Sub Form_Load ()
   RedBar.min = 0
   RedBar.max = 255
   bk = 255: title.BackColor = RGB(255, 0, 0) 'red ⇒
      background
   ForeC.Value = False
   BackC.Value = True
   RedBar.Value = bk    'set bar to show background
End Sub
```

Consider what happens when the user clicks the Text Color button. The scroll bar is displaying the background color, so you save the scroll bar setting in variable bk[3] and then make the scroll bar's value the same as that of fc, the old ForeColor:

```
Sub ForeC_Click ()
   bk = RedBar.Value   'save current bk value
   RedBar.Value = fc   'set bar to fc value
End Sub
```

A similar process is needed for Sub BackC_Click ( ):

```
Sub BackC_Click ()
   fc = RedBar.Value   'save current fc value
   RedBar.Value = bk   'set bar to bk value
End Sub
```

Depending on the option button that the user has selected, a change in the position of the slider might affect ForeColor or BackColor. The scroll bar setting must jump to the current ForeColor or BackColor setting, depending on the option button that the user has selected. To handle this, you must add an **If ... End If** structure to the Change routine:

```
Sub RedBar_Change ()
   If ForeC.Value = 0 Then        'bar is controlling Bk
      title.BackColor = RGB(RedBar.Value, 0, 0)
      redvalue = RedBar.Value
   Else                           'scroll bar is ⇒
      controlling fc
      title.ForeColor = RGB(RedBar.Value, 0, 0)
```

---

[2]This is also true in multiform applications when control (the focus) first passes to the form from another form.

[3]If the user clicks the same button twice in a row, you might think that the program would save the wrong value in bk, because the scroll bar is now controlling the ForeColor. However, Visual Basic protects against this by entering an option button Click routine only if the button's value is 0.

```
                    redvalue = RedBar.Value
          End If
      End Sub
```

Earlier in this chapter, you learned that variables are local to their own **Sub**s. But fc and bk are in several **Sub**s. To make them global to all controls' **Sub**s, add the following line to the general declarations section:

```
Dim bk, fc as integer
```

Now run your program. You should be able to display both the title and the title's background in varying intensities of black and red.

Modifications

1. The preceding instructions did not mention the use of the label redvalue on the right side of the form. At design time, you placed a zero in the label. Have the label display the scroll bar's current value. (Hint: You must use the **Str$** function to change the scroll bar value to a string.)

2. Currently you are controlling only red. Add two more scroll bars and their accompanying labels on each side for green and blue. You will have to invent some more variables. You might find it handy to use bkred rather than the current current bk, as well as bkgreen, bkblue, fcred, fcgreen, and fcblue. Just follow the pattern for the red variables. (Hint: The **RGB()** function statements will not contain zeros. The second argument is the reading on the green bar.)

Enhancement

Experiment with the scroll bars, to find the settings for black, white,[4] and all the colors of the rainbow. Create a set of buttons that enables the user to simply click a button to change colors. Figure 6-6 shows a sample form.

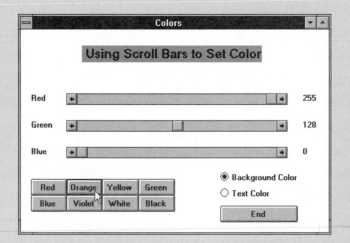

Figure 6-6
An enhanced color scroll bars program with color buttons

---

[4]For example, white is RGB(255, 255, 255).

Exercises

☐ ☐ ☐

At your desk

1. What happens to Label1 if, during the program, this statement is reached:

```
Label1.BackColor = QBColor(4)
```

2. What window do you open to select a color for Text1.ForeColor without knowing the color number?

3. What colors would the following produce?

   a. RGB(0, 0, 0) _____
   b. RGB(0, 255, 0) _____
   c. RGB(255, 0, 255) _____

4. By default, when a **Sub** is entered, the values of its variables.

   a. are set at zero
   b. become what their previous values were in that **Sub** the last time it was entered
   c. take on the value of the variables in the previous **Sub** executed

5. If you use the command **Static** in a **Sub**, what is the result?

6. You have made the following **Sub**, AddIt:

```
AddIt (a, b, c$)
```

What is wrong with each of the following statements that call the **Sub** from elsewhere in the application?

   a. AddIt
   b. AddIt a, b
   c. AddIt x, y, z
   d. AddIt November, 20, 1990

7. What property of a horizontal scroll bar determines the highest number setting that the bar can represent?

8. Which of the following statements concerning two option buttons placed in a form is *incorrect*?

   a. The option buttons can both have value **False**.
   b. The option buttons can both have value **True.**
   c. One option button can have value **True** while the other has value **False**.

At your computer

1. What is, by default, the maximum value of a horizontal scroll bar?

2. What **RGB()** statement do you use to produce the color yellow?

3. Create the application shown in Figure 6-6. The application features a vertical scroll bar that represents a thermometer. Have it range between 0 and 100 Celsius (−20 to 212 Fahrenheit). Color the form and its contents yellow. As you scroll up and down, the temperature value should display in the *text box* at the bottom right. If you enter a value in the text box, the thermometer takes on that setting.

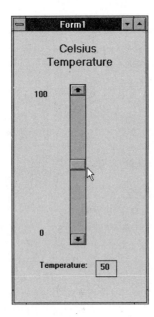

Figure 6-7
The thermometer application

Hint: Visual Basic designers obviously were not thinking of thermometers when they decided whether the top or the bottom should be Min.

What happens if you enter a number greater than the maximum value? Can you guard against the error that results?

Hint: An Out of Space error can result from an infinite loop. If a change in the text box results in a change to the scroll bar value, which results in a change to the text box value, which results in a change to the scroll bar value, which results in a change…

Chapter 7

☐ ☐ ☐

Using Option Buttons, Check Boxes, and Frames

In Chapter 6, you used two option buttons—one for a control's ForeColor and the other for the BackColor. When the user selected one option button, the other turned off. The program allowed only one choice.

But what if you want your form to require the user to select one of Automatic or Manual *and* one of 2-Door, 4-Door, or Hatchback? You have to be able to group your option buttons and make one group operate independently of the other. To handle this, you use **frames**.

Also, how can you enable a user to select *more* than one option from a single list, as you would if you were creating a computerized shopping list? For this, you need **check boxes**.

7.1 Using option buttons and check boxes

Figure 7-1 shows a sample form that surveys computer users regarding their computer use. The form has three *frames*. Each has a caption and a rectangular border. The frames on the left contain options buttons. In each of these frames, the user can choose only one of the possible selections.

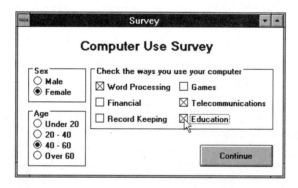

Figure 7-1
A form containing option buttons and check boxes in frames

As long as the option buttons are in the same frame, Visual Basic automatically allows only one selection and turns off a button if the user selects another. If you had placed the option buttons on the form itself or all in the same frame, selecting one of the Age options would turn off both Sex option buttons.

The largest frame contains *check boxes*. The user can select more than one of these options.

The *Value* property of an option button and a check box shows whether the user has selected it. For the application shown in Figure 7-1, FemaleOption.Value would be **True** (–1) and MaleOption.Value would be **False** (0). Check box values work a little differently; each check box has the value +1.[1]

7.2 Using frames

To separate sets of option buttons and make each set independent of the other, you must place each set in its own frame. Start by selecting the frame button and placing the frame on the form just as you place any other control (by using the drag-and-release method). If necessary, you can move and resize the frame. Then, with the frame selected (that is, with the handles showing), add your controls in the frame, taking each *directly* from the toolbar to the frame.

You must be careful to place controls *into* a frame not *on top of* the frame. For example, you cannot first create an option button on the form, make the frame, and then move the button into (onto) the frame. The control would then be *in front of* the frame, not *in it.* To place any control inside a frame, you must first make the frame.

If you want to place an existing control inside the frame, select the control, choose Cut from the Edit menu, select the frame, and choose Paste from the Edit menu. The object appears in the frame's top-left corner, but you can move it to any position you want.

You can put any control into a frame, including labels, buttons, and text boxes. An advantage of this capability is that you can move the controls as a group simply by moving the frame. Often, many of these controls are the same size. A quick way to create them is to use the Copy command.

7.3 Using Copy and Paste to create similar controls

Suppose that you have several text boxes to place on your frame. You want them initially to be empty, perhaps colored, and all the same size. To avoid having to change all the properties for each box, you should use the following technique. Make the first box. Set its properties (Size, Color, Name, FontSize, Caption or Text, and so on). From the Edit menu, choose Copy and then Paste. Visual Basic will display the question shown in Figure 7-2. (The name in quotation marks varies depending on the particular control that you copy.)

---

[1] A selected check box has the value +1, but a selected option button has the value –1. Although this apparent inconsistency is unfortunate, you simply must remember that True and False work with option buttons, and 1 and 0 with check boxes.

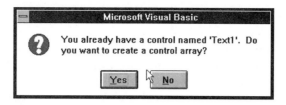

Figure 7-2
The question that you must answer when you paste a control

Usually you click No. Visual Basic then assigns a new name (such as Text2, if no other control already has that name) to the pasted control. If you answer Yes, you will have two controls with the same name: a **control array**. They will have different **indices**. You learn about arrays in Chapter 9.

If you accidentally answer Yes, you eventually see the error message shown in Figure 7-3. If you look in the properties list for the control, you will see an index value. Even removing the value and changing control names may not fix the problem. You will find it quicker and less frustrating just to delete the controls that have index values and then recreate them.

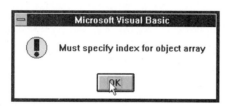

Figure 7-3
The message displayed when a control array is missing an index

7.4 Detecting pushed option buttons

All option buttons in a frame work as a unit. When one option button is selected, the others are not. To make this scheme work, Visual Basic uses **True** and **False** values. (For Visual Basic 1, **True** is equal to –1 and **False** to 0.) The selected button in the frame has value equal to **True** and the others have values equal to **False**. Therefore, the code that you write to determine which option button is selected usually looks like the following:

```
If Option1.Value = True Then   'or whatever option ⇒
  button was called
    do something
Else
    do something else
End If
```

7.5 Detecting checked check boxes

You might think that Visual Basic check boxes would register **True** or **False** values like option values. Unfortunately, this isn't the case. Unlike the selected option button's value of –1 (**True**), a checked box has the value +1. Both unselected option buttons and unchecked check boxes have the value 0.

Application 7

Letting the user set the options

Overview

When this program starts, a window appears asking the user to enter a title for the form. The user can select various options to change the way that the title is displayed.

Learning objectives

- using frames
- using option buttons
- using check boxes
- using InputBox$
- changing between upper- and lowercase and italics, bold, and normal
- using a general **Sub**
- defining variables in general declarations
- setting initial conditions in Form_Load

Instructions

The form contains a label called Title, two frames, and two command buttons, New Title and End. One frame contains three check boxes, and the other three option buttons. Figure 7-4 shows the form.

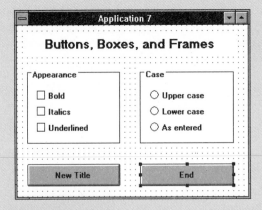

Figure 7-4
The form for Application 7

The title's FontSize is 13.5. Notice that Visual Basic sets FontBold to **True** when you choose this font size.

Before creating any buttons or check boxes, select the frame button from the toolbar and make two frames. Then place the buttons and check boxes in the frames. Drag each one far enough that you can display the caption. The buttons have the control names Upperoption, Loweroption, and Asoption; the check boxes have the names Boldcheck, Italicscheck, and Underlinecheck.

When the program starts, a dialog box appears asking the user to enter a different title for the form. To display this dialog box, you use **InputBox$**, a built-in dialog box similar to **MsgBox$**. You want to display this dialog box when the form loads and when the user presses the New Title button. Instead of writing the same code twice, create a **Sub** called GetTitle. Go to any code window (by double-clicking on the form, for example) and type the following:

```
Sub GetTitle ()
  entry$ = InputBox$(prompt$, "", default$)
  If entry$ = "" Then entry$ = "Buttons, Boxes, and ⇒
    Frames"
  Title.Caption = entry$          'place this in the ⇒
    Title label
  default$ = entry$               'save for default next time
End Sub
```

The first line of GetTitle shows the syntax of **InputBox$**. Following the parenthesis comes the instruction to the user, a title for the box itself, and a default entry that the program will place in the box's text input area.

Allowing an empty title defeats the purpose of this application, so the second line creates a title if necessary.

The application calls GetTitle from Form_Load, which first defines the initial prompt and default:

```
Sub Form_Load ()
  prompt$ = "Enter a title for the form."
  default$ = "Buttons, Boxes, and Frames"
  GetTitle
End Sub
```

GetTitle appears in the code for the New Title button:

```
Sub NewTitleButton
  GetTitle
End Sub
```

Remember that variables are local to (known only by) the Subs in which they appear, and that their values are not normally passed from one Sub to another. But because you want GetTitle to know what prompt$ and default$ are, As shown in Figure 7-5, you dimension them in general declarations. All Subs in the form will share these variables.

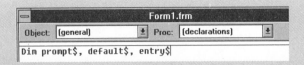

Figure 7-5
Making variables common throughout the form

Double-click on each of the option buttons in turn and add the following code:

```
Sub Loweroption_Click ()
    Title.caption = Lcase$(entry$)        'lowercase ⇒
       equivalent of entry$
End Sub

Sub Upperoption_Click ()
    Title.caption = Ucase$(entry$)        'uppercase ⇒
       equivalent of entry$
End Sub
```

Note that entry$ itself does not change in either of the preceding routines. (The variable never appears on the left side of an equals sign.) Thus you can return to the original entry$ when the user clicks the As Entered option button:

```
Sub Asoption_Click ()
    Title.caption = entry$
End Sub
```

Add the following code for your check boxes:

```
Sub Boldcheck_Click ()
    If Boldcheck.Value = 1 Then
      Title.FontBold = True
    Else
      Title.FontBold = False
    End If
End Sub

Sub Italicscheck_Click ()
    If Italicscheck.Value = 1 Then
      Title.FontItalic = True
    Else
      Title.FontItalic = False
    End If
End Sub

Sub Underlinecheck_Click ()
    If Underlinecheck.Value = 1 Then
      Title.FontUnderline = True
    Else
```

```
                              Title.FontUnderline = False
                    End If
                End Sub
```

When using check boxes and option buttons, you should always set the initial conditions (for example, which button you want the application to select by default) in Form_Load. You can activate Asoption, and make sure that FontBold, FontItalic, and FontUnderline are set to **False**. Add these lines to the bottom of Form_Load, after GetTitle:

```
'set initial conditions
    Boldcheck.Value = 0: Title.FontBold = False
    Italicscheck.Value = 0: Title.FontItalic = False
    Underlinecheck.Value = 0: Title.FontUnderline = ⇒
        False
    Asoption.Value = True: Title.Caption = entry$
```

Why didn't you have to define the other two option values, Upperoption.Value and Loweroption.Value?

After you code the End button, you can run the program.

Modifications

1. Putting some controls on frames enables you to link them physically. To see how this works, try rearranging your form by dragging the frames around. Note that the buttons and check boxes move with them.

2. Add a frame that contains options for coloring the title's text. You could, for example, enable the title to be red, green, blue, or black. You could use the **RGB()** numbers for these colors, find the hex values using the color palette, or use **QBColor()**. The code for red could be as follows:

```
Title.ForeColor = QBColor(4)
```

Enhancement

You might have noticed that the **InputBox$** appears over whatever background your computer happens to be running. This can result in quite a cluttered screen. When a program starts, the Form_Load routines run first, then Form_Paint draws the form. If you put the code currently in Form_Load into Form_Paint, the form would appear on the screen first, followed by the **InputBox$**. Try it. Perhaps this isn't much of an improvement. Try making your form full-screen, or at least much bigger, so that **InputBox$** stands out more clearly. The form might look better off-center; try adding an x and y value inside the parentheses:

```
original = InputBox$(prompt$, title$, default$, ⇒
    xvalue, yvalue)
```

Experiment with different x and y values. You'll find that when the startup code is in Form_Paint, you might fall into an infinite loop and have to exit the program from the Run menu or by pressing **Ctrl+Break**. Don't leave the program this way!

Exercises

At your desk

1. State the differences between option buttons and check boxes in the following categories:

   a.   icon
   b.   appearance
   c.   value when selected or checked
   d.   behavior

2. If you create a frame, place a new button inside it, and move the frame, what happens to the button?

3. You are designing a computer chess game. You want to enable the user to pick his or her own color (white or black). Would you use option buttons or check boxes? Why?

4. From a list of players in a hockey game, you want the user to select the three stars (the best players). Would you use option buttons or check boxes? Why?

5. To choose the Major League Baseball all-star team, fans make their selections on cards that list about 10 choices for each position on the team. For infield positions, you can choose one catcher, one shortstop, one firstbaseman, and so on. You can choose the three outfielders from a longer list. To implement this procedure on the computer screen, you would need option buttons, check boxes, *and* frames. Explain why you would need all three, and where you would use each. (You do not need to understand baseball to answer this question. All clues are in the description of the card.)

6. In Application 7, why did only four of the six controls inside the frames have to be set in Form_Load?

At your computer

Create the order form shown in Figure 7-6. Each time that the user clicks on an option button or check box, the price changes. Make the starting configuration (that is, the one that appears when you start the application and after you press the New Order button) a small, delivered pizza with no toppings.

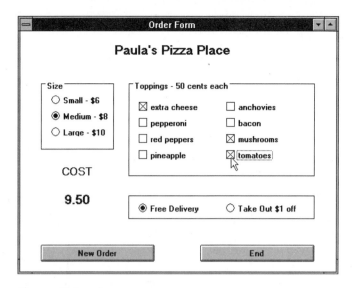

Figure 7-6
The Order Form application

You may have difficulty displaying the final zeros in the cost. Assuming that the application is displaying the cost in costlabel, and total is the variable that holds the pizza's cost, the following code line will solve the problem:

```
costlabel.caption = Format$(total,"##.00")
```

To see how this solution works, look up **Format$** in Help. Here's a hint:

```
sizecost = -6 * (small) + -8 * (medium) + -10 * (large)
```

Why the negative signs? Check the Help screens.

Chapter 8 Using Loops, List Boxes, and Combo Boxes

Computers are excellent at doing repetitive tasks. The code for calculating the balance on your mortgage on February 1, given January's starting balance, interest rate, and payment, is simple. But after you write the code, you certainly want the computer to repeat the process for the remaining 11 months of the year instead of writing the same statements 11 more times. To repeat the process, you need a **loop**, which is a routine that enables you to repeat a series of statements.

8.1 Loops: doing something many times

You can use two types of loops: **For ... Next** and **Do ... Loop**.

For ... Next loops

To make a beep on the computer's speaker, you just say so:

```
Beep
```

Beep is actually a useful command. You can use it to alert to the user to a new message that you have placed on the screen. Or, while designing and testing a program, you can put the statement after a line or in a **Sub** and then simply listen to hear whether the program made it to that line of code.

To make 10 beeps, you can simply write **Beep** 10 times. However, you can also use a **For ... Next** loop:

```
For i = 1 To 10 'do something 10 times, with i going 1, ⇒
  2, 3 ... to 10
  Beep
Next I     'i increases here. If 10 or less, program ⇒
  loops back.
```

The preceding loop might look more complicated than 10 **Beep** lines, but has the advantage of flexibility. Suppose that you want the user to choose the number of beeps by typing a number into a text box. To do this, you could use the following code:

```
numberoftimes = Val(text1.text)     'this will be the ⇒
  number of beeps
For i = 1 To numberoftimes
  Beep
Next i
```

Thus a **For ... Next** loop has the following structure:

```
For countervariable = startingnumber To endingnumber
   ...
   do something (could be many lines of code)
   ...
Next countervariable
```

The **Next** line increases the `countervariable` by one (in this case). The loop keeps repeating, and `countervariable` keeps increasing each time the loop reaches the **Next** statement. The program exits the loop (that is, it stops repeating) when the `countervariable` exceeds `endingnumber`.

Suppose that you want to add the numbers 1 to 5. Use a **For ... Next** loop to add the numbers one at a time to a variable initialized to zero:

```
total = 0
For i = 1 To 5
   total = total + i
Next i
```

In a more likely example, you might want to prompt the user to supply some data. To request five numbers and calculate an average, you can use the same structure, except that you add a line to wait for and accept the user's input:

```
total = 0
for i = 1 To 5
   prompt$ = "Enter number" + str$(i)   'e.g. When i = 1 ⇒
      "Enter number 1"
   number = val(inputBox(prompt$))
   total = total + number
next i
average = total / 5
```

You use **For ... Next** loops when your program knows, before entering the loop, how many repetitions to make (even if the upper or lower limit is the value of a variable).

Do ... Loops

Often you don't know in advance how many times a program is going to repeat a section. This usually happens because the program will repeat some statements until the user does something or until some variable reaches a significant value. For example, the following routine plays a game until the user chooses a No button:

```
Do
   ...
   ...play the game
   ...
   button = MsgBox("Play again?",36) '(a box with Yes and ⇒
      No buttons)
```

```
     Loop Until button = 7          '7 means "No" was pressed
```

When the computer reaches the **Loop** instruction, which happens if the user does *not* choose the No button, the program loops back and repeats the action that it began under the **Do** statement.

Here is how you might use a **Do ... Loop** to continue asking for a password until the user gets it right:

```
pass$ = ""    'clear out pass$ in case it already ⇒
  equals password$
Do until pass$ = password$     'set up exit condition
  pass$ = InputBox("Enter password")     'request a ⇒
    password
Loop
```

Maybe you should allow only three tries. In the following example, notice that the programmer has placed a condition in the **Do** statement and added a statement to count the number of times that the loop repeats:

```
tries = 0                      'reset try counter
pass$ = ""                     'clear out pass$
Do Until pass$ = password$ or tries = 3  'set up exit ⇒
  condition
  pass$ = InputBox("Enter password")
  tries = tries + 1                      'increase tries
Loop
If pass$<> password$ Then MsgBox "Wrong Password", 16, ⇒
  "Good-bye" : End
```

Note that the last line uses the **MsgBox** *statement*, while the previous use of **MsgBox** (in Chapter 3) was the **MsgBox** *function*. The function *returns a value*, so it begins with somenumber = MsgBox. The **MsgBox** statement simply displays the message. Note also that the **MsgBox** statement has no parentheses.

> The preceding password routines are not ideal. Their purpose is strictly to demonstrate how a **Do ... Loop** works. You would never use **InputBox** to take in a user's password, because the screen would then display the password as the user types it. In Programming Adventure 2, you will create a better password routine.

8.2 ASCII values

Computers can manipulate text, but when they do so they are actually working with numbers. Computer hardware and software manufacturers have adopted a standard convention, the ASCII character set, that defines a number between 1 and 255 for the characters that you can type at the keyboard. The ASCII set also includes some other characters that are often useful, including some symbols, graphics characters, and foreign letters.

In this chapter's application program, you use the ASCII number for the Enter key: 13. Although you can always look up the ASCII character numbers in tables[1] in your manual, the characters listed in Table 8.1 are worth memorizing.

Table 8.1 Four of the Most Critical ASCII Characters

Key	ASCII	Character
Enter	13	A character at the end of a paragraph or line; also called Return (from typewriter's carriage return).
Line Feed	10	A character that causes the cursor to move down a line.
Space	32	A blank character such as that between two words. (For example, "The End" is a seven character long string.)
Quote (")	34	Quotation marks. You must include these characters within strings. To make a$ equal to **"Hello," she said**, you must enter the following: **a$ = chr$(34)+"Hello,"+ chr$(34)+" she said"**

8.3 Creating list boxes and combo boxes

Figure 8-1 shows a window that contains both a list and a combo box. The programmer defines the list box's height. A combo box is a list box that remains closed until the user clicks on the arrow; then the combo box drops down to display a list of choices. A combo box, depending on its type, or **style**, can also enable the user to enter an unlisted choice from the keyboard, making the combo box a combination of a list box and a text box.

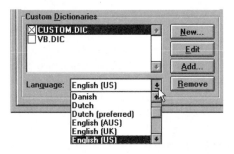

Figure 8-1
A list box (Custom Dictionaries) and a combo box (Language)

List boxes and combo boxes enable the user to select from a set of choices. This section describes their most important features. As you read this section, enter the short examples on your computer.

List boxes

Create the form shown in Figure 8-2. It contains a list box and two buttons.

---

[1] In Chapter 10, you develop a small application that displays on-screen the ASCII numbers of keys.

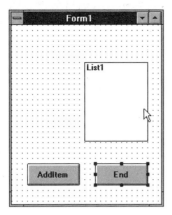

Figure 8-2
A list box example

Then declare a global variable in general declarations:

```
Dim ynow as integer
```

In Form_Load, set the scale's width and height and initialize ynow:

```
Sub Form_Load ()
    scaleheight = 1000
    scalewidth = 2000
    ynow = 200          'initial value
End Sub
```

Now create a button called AddButton. Then make a list box. Just use the default name List1.

To see how a list box works, add the following code to AddButton and to List1_DblClick (not Click):

```
Sub AddButton_Click ()
   List1.AddItem "Item " + Str$(List1.ListCount)
End Sub

Sub List1_DblClick ()
   xnow = 120
   ynow = ynow + 50   'down a line
   CurrentX = xnow: CurrentY = ynow
   Print "Item " + List1.ListIndex
End Sub
```

Two properties of the list boxes illustrated in the code are ListCount, the number of items in the list, and ListIndex, the item highlighted (with the top item being item zero). The following is the method for adding an item to the list:

```
List1.Additem "some string"
```

Run the program to test it. Add many items to the list and see how the scroll bars appear. What happens if you select an item from the list with a single click and use the cursor arrow keys? Would you like to be able to select an item by pressing Enter? To make pressing Enter have the same result as double-clicking a selection, you can check for the Enter key:

```
Sub List1_KeyDown (KeyCode As Integer, Shift As Integer)
   If KeyCode = 13 Then List1_DblClick
End Sub
```

Combo boxes

A combo box is a list box with a text box at the top. The FontSize pulldown menu in the Visual Basic properties list is an example; you can select from the list or enter from the keyboard a font size value at the top.

The following is a simple example that includes a combo box, a label, and an EndButton.

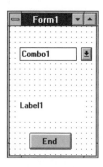

Figure 8-3
A combo box example

Create the following Subs:

```
Sub Form_Load ()
   Combo1.Text = ""        'clear the display
   Combo1.AddItem "milk"   'start with two items
   Combo1.AddItem "bread"
End Sub

Sub Combo1_Click ()
   Label1.Caption = "Bring home " + Combo1.Text
End Sub

Sub Combo1_KeyDown (KeyCode As Integer, Shift As ⇒
   Integer)
   If KeyCode = 13 Then  'Enter was pressed
      Combo1.AddItem Combo1.Text    'Add whatever was ⇒
      typed
```

```
        Label1.Caption = "Bring home " + Combo1.Text ⇒
          'Display it
        Combo1.Text = ""              'Wipe the top of the box
      End If
  End Sub
```

Combo boxes have a Style property. Set the Style to 0 (the drop-down combo box). You can select this style from the pulldown menu or by entering a new string at the top. The Combo1_KeyDown routine, on detecting the pressing of the Enter key, adds the item to the list box and displays the choice.

What happens if you successively press Enter? Do you see the blank entries added to the list? Adding a check for a blank entry helps:

```
    ... If KeyCode = 13 and Combo1.Text <> "" Then
```

Experiment with the other combo box styles. You will find that Style 1 (a simple combo box) is little more than a text box. Style 2 (the drop-down list) does not allow changes to the text at the top of the box. You must remove lines of code that attempt to clear the text. Because the user is not to add items by typing, you must also remove the lines that process the Enter key.

Application 8 — List and combo boxes

Although this application is not terribly useful, it does demonstrate the important techniques for employing list and combo boxes in your applications.

Overview

When the program starts, a list box with five phrases and a combo box with five random numbers appears. The user can select from each list, add entries, or clear the box.

Learning objectives

- setting initial conditions when the program begins

- changing text to a value

- using Do ... While loops

- using For ... Next loops

- using list and combo boxes

- using AddItem and RemoveItem methods

- generating random numbers

- using Format$ to display numbers

Instructions

Figure 8-4 shows this application's form.

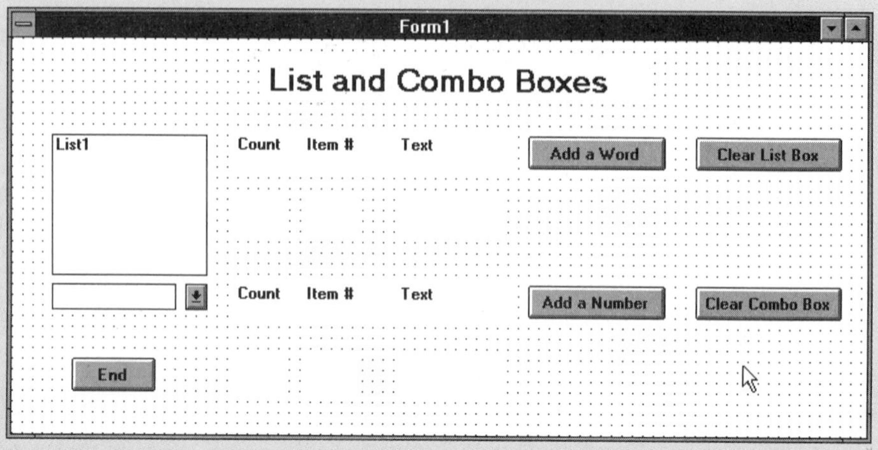

Figure 8-4
A form with a list box, combo box, five buttons, and nine labels

Beside the list box are four labels. The wide box next to the list box (List 1) contains the headings for the three labels underneath: LCount, LItem, and LText. Under the headings for the labels next to the combo box (Combo 1) are the labels CCount, CItem, and CText. The buttons are called ListAddButton, ListClearButton, ComboAddButton, ComboClearButton, and EndButton.

When the form loads, the application places five items into List1 and five random numbers (between 0 and 1) into Combo1:

```
Sub Form_Load ()
  For i = 1 To 5        '5 repetitions
    List1.AddItem "Word" + Str$(i)  'add to the list
  Next i

  LCount.Caption = Str$(List1.ListCount)     'display ⇒
    number of items

  For i = 1 To 5
    Combo1.AddItem Format$(Rnd, .#00)  'add random ⇒
        #, 3 decimal places
  Next i

  CCount.Caption = Str$(Combo1.ListCount)

End Sub
```

List1.AddItem adds the string that follows it to the bottom of the list. However, if you set the Sorted property to **True**, the word will go to its proper alphabetical place.

*The period between the control name and the word AddItem makes AddItem look like a property. However, this impression is incorrect; AddItem is not on the properties list. Visual Basic calls the AddItem operation a **method**. (It's too bad Microsoft didn't use some other* *punctuation here, such as List1~AddItem.) Regardless of its name or punctuation, to add to a list box called List1, you use the following statement:*

```
List1.AddItem "something"
```

When the user clicks on the list box, the application displays the selected item:

```
Sub List1_Click ()
   LItem.Caption = Str$(List1.ListIndex+1)
   LText.Caption = List1.Text
End Sub
```

A list box's ListIndex property is a number that corresponds to the position of a selected item. The first item in a list box is item 0. If a list box has no items, ListIndex is –1. The preceding code adds 1 to the item number to be displayed. You increment this item because only computer programmers accept that lists can start with item 0; normal humans expect the first item to be item 1.

The ListCount property does start with 1, so the property is the exact number of items in the list. The ListAddButton_Click code records the number, adds a phrase that includes the next number, and updates the display:

```
Sub ListAddButton_Click ()
   n = List1.ListCount
   List1.AddItem "New Word" + Str$(n + 1)
   LCount.Caption = Str$(List1.ListCount)
End Sub
```

Combo1's click routine is similar:

```
Sub Combo1_Click ()
   CItem.Caption = Str$(Combo1.ListIndex + 1)
   CText.Caption = Combo1.Text
End Sub
```

Use the List1.RemoveItem method in a loop to remove all items from the list:

```
Sub ListClearButton_Click ()
   For i = 1 to List1.ListCount
      List1.RemoveItem 0        'always remove first item
   Next i
   LCount.Caption = "0"
   LItem.Caption = ""
   LText.Caption = ""
End Sub
```

The lines after the loop update the screen display by erasing any displayed word and announcing that the list has no items.

Do you see why you always remove item 0? After you remove the first one, the former item 1 (the second one down) is now item 0, the old item 2 is now item 1, and so on.

You could have used a different kind of loop. Try it in Combo1's clear routine:

```
Sub ComboClearButton_Click ()
   Do While Combo1.ListCount > 0  'while there is ⇒
      something there ...
      Combo1.RemoveItem 0                  'remove it
   Loop

   CCount.Caption = "0"
   CItem.Caption = ""
   CText.Caption = ""
End Sub
```

Words or numbers in the top display portion of the combo box are called Combo1.Text. When the user chooses the Add a Number button, the application adds to the list any text in Combo1.Text and displays the new entry:

```
Sub ComboAddButton_Click ()
   Combo1.AddItem Combo1.Text                 'add to list
   CCount.Caption = Str$(Combo1.ListCount) 'new count
    CText.Caption = Combo1.Text                 'show this ⇒
        new last item
   CItem.Caption = Str$(Combo1.ListCount)  'show that it ⇒
      is at bottom
End Sub
```

Figure 8-5 shows the application in use. The user has just added a new number and then pulled down the combo box to see whether it lists the number.

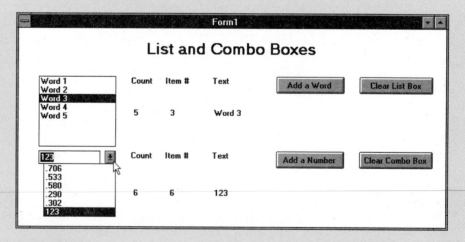

Figure 8-5
The running application

Modification

What if the user clicks the Add a Number button when no text is entered at the top of the combo box? Pull down the list and see what's happening. Fix it with an **If** statement in the ComboAddButton_Click routine.

Enhancements

1. Most touch typists would prefer to type data and press **Enter** instead of reaching for the mouse to click on the Add a Number button. Check for the pressing of the **Enter** key when the cursor is active in the combo box. You will look for a keycode of 13 in Sub Combo1_KeyDown.

2. Check also for the **Esc** key, which typists might press to clear any of their typing. The key's keycode is 27.

Exercises

At your desk

1. How many beeps will you hear in each of the following examples?

   a.
   ```
   For x = 1 To 5
      Beep
   Next x
   ```

   b.
   ```
   For x = 1 To 5
       For j = 1 To 3
           Beep
       Next j
   Next x
   ```

   c.
   ```
   For x = 1 To 5
       For j = x To 3
           Beep
       Next j
   Next x
   ```

2. What is the value of abc at the end of the following loop?

   ```
   count = 0 : abc = 0
   Do
       count = count + 1
       abc = abc + count
   Loop Until count > 3
   ```

3. The letters A to D are separate line items in a list box. If you remove item 2, which letters remain?

4. You have a list box called Food. What statement adds the item Bread to the list box?

5. Write the *three lines* of code for setting up a combo box called CBox with the even numbers 2 to 10, as shown in Figure 8-6.

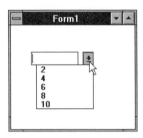

Figure 8-6
The combo box CBox

At your computer

Create the application shown in Figure 8-7. The message should change depending on the user's choices. Note that the form consists of different types of boxes.

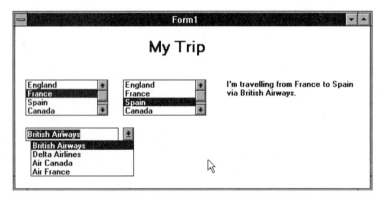

Figure 8-7
The My Trip application

Chapter 9 Using Arrays

Many applications must keep track of a large number of similar items, such as 24 teams' scores, 30 students' marks, 100 book titles, or the names of all your friends. If your program is to keep all these items in memory at the same time, you need one variable for each item. Arrays provide the way to manipulate many similar items *without* inventing a different variable name for each one. In this chapter, you learn the two types of arrays: arrays of variables and arrays of controls..

9.1 Variable arrays

You can use both one-dimensional and multidimensional variable arrays.

One-dimensional arrays

Suppose that you want to keep track of five different prices and calculate the total. You could use five different variables, as in the following two examples:

```
total = a + b + c + d + e
total = price1 + price2 + price3 + price4 + price5
```

This method has several drawbacks. What if you had a hundred prices rather than five? You would need quite a long line to write down all the variable names. Also, how could you make your program flexible? That is, how could you enable the user to determine how many prices to add if you have "hardwired" the number of variables in the coding?

A better way is to use an array to keep track of the prices. An array variable has a number (or numeric variable) in parentheses after an otherwise conventional variable name. You use `price(1)` for the first price, `price(2)` for the next, and so on, all the way to `price(n)`, where n is any number that you or the user determines.[1] The routine that calculates the total looks like this:

```
total = 0
for i=1 to n
    total = total + price(i)
next i
```

`Price(i)` is the ith price. Think of an array as a set of similar variables all with the same name but with different **indices**. (In QBasic, the *i* is the **subscript**. In Visual Basic, it is called the **index**.)[2]

---

[1] If you have a mathematics background, you will be familiar with the concept of subscripted variables: x_1, y_1, x_2, y_2. Array notation is similar, except that the subscripts are placed in parentheses: x(1), y(1), x(2), y(2).

[2] Some throwbacks to QBasic teminology remain in Visual Basic. If your "index" takes on an improper value, Visual Basic gives you a "Subscript out of range" error message.

Before you first use an array variable, you must **dimension** it. This informs the computer how many memory locations to set aside for your array. You dimension the array by specifying the highest possible index that you will use. This is done in one of two ways:

If you wish the array to be global array, available to all **Subs** in the form, you dimension the array in general declarations.

```
Dim price(100)³
```

Dimensioning the array in general declarations is the usual practice. If, however, you wish to use the array only in one **Sub** you can use **ReDim** in that individual Sub instead:

```
Sub DisplayPrices ( )
   ReDim price(100)
   ... 'the rest of the code for this Sub
End Sub
```

Here is an example. Suppose that you want four different counters, each of which increases depending on a user's selection. In the following example, you use **InputBox** to accept the user's choice:

```
Dim counter(4)  '(in general declarations)
...
choice = 0
Do Until choice >= 1 And choice <= 4   'wait for ⇒
   suitable number
     prompt$ = "Increase which? (Enter a number between ⇒
       1 and 4)."
     choice = InputBox prompt$
Loop
counter(choice) = counter(choice) + 1 'increase that one
```

You could print the values using the following code:

```
For i = 1 To 4
   PRINT counter(i)     'print on the form ... (not ⇒
     discussed yet!)
Next i
```

You could display the values in a **control array** (discussed in Section 9-2):

```
For i = 1 To 4
   label1(i).Caption = Str$(counter(i))
Next i
```

Multidimensional arrays

Arrays with one index are one-dimensional (1-D) arrays. You can have arrays with more than one index. You can also use two one-dimensional arrays to store points on a graph, x(1) and y(1) for the x and y coordinates of the first point. Alternatively,

---

³The example Dim price(100) actually gives you 101 prices, because there is a price(0).

you could use a two-dimensional (2-D) array. The x value of the ith point that you are about to plot on a graph could be `Position(i,0)` and the y value `Position(i,1)`. For example, if the 10th point is the point (50, 100), then `Position(10, 0) = 50` and `Position(10, 1) = 100`.

Suppose that you are keeping a computer inventory. Your store has 100 items, so you could dimension two arrays to store prices:

```
Dim wholesale(100), retail(100)
```

You could do this in one array:

```
Dim item(100,2)
```

This way, `item(50, 1)` would be the wholesale price of the 50th item, and `item(50,2)` could be the item's retail price. You could even define two constants:

```
Const whole = 1, retail = 2
```

Then you don't have to remember which is which: `item(1, whole)` is the wholesale price of the first item, and `item(1, retail)` is the retail price of the first item.

Usually, deciding whether to use two 1-D arrays or a single 2-D arrays is a matter of your convenience. Either way, you need the same number of memory locations to store the two prices for all 100 items.

Some applications demand even larger arrays. For example, a program for storing student marks might use the folllowing line:

```
x = mark(student, item, category, term)
```

That is, `mark( 5, 7, 3, 2)` could be the fifth student's seventh test mark (tests being evaluation category 3) in the second term.

Two dimensions are about all that most programmers want to deal with!

9.2 Control arrays

The arrays you have seen so far are variable arrays–a single variable name representing more than one item, each with its own index. The fact that you use variables in not apparent to the user, because variables and the rest of the program's code work in the background. The user does, however, see the controls on the form. Many of your programs will have sets of controls that look and act similarly, such as a series of text boxes or labels. You want to use controls as arrays so that, as with variable arrays, you can give each the same name but a different index.

Suppose that you are displaying the names of 10 different people on your form, each in its own label. You are keeping the names in your program in an array called `person$()`. You would start with the following Dim statement:

```
Dim person$(10)
```

Suppose that your program then goes through a loop and uses **InputBox** to take in the names. person$(1) is the first name, person$(2) the second name, and so on. Now you want to put the names into 10 different text boxes. Is the following code efficient for this purpose?

```
Personbox1.text = person$(1)
Personbox2.text = person$(2)
Personbox3.text = person$(3)
...
Personbox10.text = person$(10)
```

Of course, there's a better way. Just as you have an array, person, to hold 10 different names, you can have an array of controls, each with the same name but a different index. Do you remember when you copied a text box and pasted it? Visual Basic warned you that you were about to create a control with the same name as another control (see Figure 9-1). You answered No to the question and Visual Basic named the pasted control Text2.

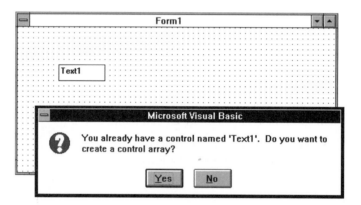

Figure 9-1
A warning that two controls have the same name

If you answer Yes to the question, the pasted control receives the same name. The result of an affirmative answer to the question in Figure 9-1 is a new text box also called Text1. This text box would have index 1. The original Text1, which before had no index at all, would now have an index 0.

In the persons' names example, you want display the names in 10 different text boxes. You name the first box Personbox. You then copy the box and paste nine more copies onto the form (answering Yes to the question in Figure 9-1 each time), creating a control array. You now have a set of boxes, all called Personbox, with indices from 0 to 9.

Figure 9-2 shows the properties of the 10th text box. Note that the captions are still Text1 because the programmer did not change the default caption before starting the copy and paste procedure. You can see at the bottom of the properties list that the text box's name is Personbox. The Index property is 9 and the top window shows that this text box is called Personbox(9). The index is 9 because the first box now is Personbox(0).

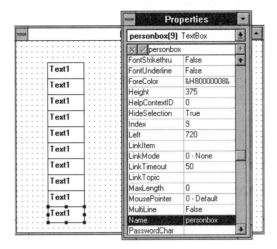

Figure 9-2
The properties list for the 10th list box

To fill your 10 text boxes with the 10 names that you have in your `person$()` array, you use the following code:

```
for i = 1 to 10
   Personbox(i - 1).text = person$(i)
next i
```

The `i - 1` is necessary because the indices of the `person$` array go from 1 to 10, but those of the control array, the array of Personbox text boxes, goes from 0 to 9.[4] The `i - 1` ensures that `Personbox(0)`, which is the first text box that you created, gets the first name, `person$(1)`.

Suppose that the user changes the name in `Personbox(6)`. You then must change what is stored in `person$(7)`. To do so, you use the Personbox_Change routine:

```
Sub Personbox_Change (index as Integer)
   person$(index + 1) = Personbox(index).text
End Sub
```

After the **Sub** name, you see the words `index as integer` in parentheses. Recall that variables are local to their **Sub** procedure. But the **Sub** and the form pass between each other the values of those variables that appear in an event's *argument list*. The argument list after the name of the **Sub** shows that *index*, the number that shows which particular Personbox control has been changed, is being passed from the form to the **Sub** procedure. The value of `person$(index + 1)` gets changed.

---

[4]To make your text boxes range from `Personbox(1)` to `Personbox(10)`, create 11 text boxes for the 10 names and then delete the first one. That way, the index for the text box matches the index for the array of names. (However, this chapter's discussion of the Personbox example assumes that you did *not* do this.)

9.3 **String functions**

To examine a string of text that a user entered, you can compare it to any pattern of characters, just as you would two numbers. The following statement looks for a match between the contents of Namebox.text and a target string, "Aladdin," and acts accordingly:

```
If Namebox.text = "Aladdin" Then greetings.Caption = ⇒
   "Hello, master"
```

This statement finds only perfect matches—the same letters, same length, same case. But Visual Basic also has functions—**Left**$, **Right**$, and **Mid**$—that can examine portions of a string. In the following examples, see if you can determine what each of these functions do. The first example uses Left$:

```
If Left$(entry$, 1) = "A" Then
   info.Caption = "You began with a capital A"
Else
   info.Caption = ""          'erase info.Caption
End If
```

The following example is similar to the previous one, but displays the *A* in the message in quotation marks. The example demonstrates a use for ASCII values, with **Chr$(34)** specifying a character with the ASCII value 34.

```
If Left$(entry$, 1) = "A" Then
   info.Caption = "Starts with an " + Chr$(34) +"A" + ⇒
     Chr$(34)
Else
   info.Caption = ""
End If
```

Left$(entry$, 1) is the first, leftmost character of entry$. You can examine more than one character. Left$(name$,3) is the first three letters of name$:

```
If Left$(name$, 3) = "Mr. " then greeting.Caption = ⇒
   "Dear Sir"
```

You can check whether the string ends with *s*:

```
If Right$(entry$, 1) = "s" Then info.Caption = ⇒
   "possibly plural"
```

Right$(a$, x) would be the last x characters of a$, where x is a number less than or equal to the length of a$.

To look at the middle of a string, you can use **Mid$**. The middle three characters of a$, starting at position 2, would be **Mid$(a$, 2, 3)**.

Track through the following code and predict what it does and how it works. The descriptive variable names tell the story, but try to understand the logic:

```
space = 0
howlong = Len(a$)      'Len = the length function = ⇒
   number of characters
For i = 1 To howlong
   If Mid$(a$, i, 1) = " " Then space = space + 1
Next i
Is space = 0 Then
   answer.Caption = "All one word"
Else
   answer.Caption = "It's made up of " + ⇒
      Str$ (space + 1) + "words."
End If
```

9.4 Covering all the possibilities

To be a good computer programmer, you must be a good problem solver. But finding the answer to a puzzle yourself is the easiest part of programming. For example, counting words in a sentence is simple. You can sort numbers in numerical order without thinking hard. It doesn't take long to state the remainder when you divide 4 into 15.

It is more difficult to explain, if only to yourself, how to make the computer do these tasks. Just *how do* you find the remainder when you divide 4 into 15? You do it easily, almost without thinking. But what are the actual steps?

So after having figured out the precise method of accomplishing a task, you write the Visual Basic statements to enable the computer to do it. But you are still not done. Your most troublesome task is to write code that enables the program to cope with the unexpected. In a word-counting example in Section 9-3, would the answer be correct if a$ started with a space? Such errors can easily occur, because a user might accidentally press the spacebar and such spaces are difficult to spot. One too many spaces results in an incorrect word count.

The following routine strips leading spaces from a$:

```
Do While Left$(a$, 1) = " " And Len(a$) <> 0
    a$ = Right$(a$, len(a$)-1)
Loop
```

Try using this routine and tracking how it strips the spaces. Start with a$ = "*space space* ABC".

The following routine also works:

```
Do While Left$(a$, 1) = " " And Len(a$) <> 0
    a$ = mid$(a$, 2)
Loop
```

Usually the **Mid$** function has three arguments: the string, the starting position, and the number of characters. You can omit the last number if you mean "all the way to the end." **Mid$(a$, 2)** means the middle of a$, starting at position 2, then all the rest of the characters.

However, another Visual Basic function does strip leading spaces, removing the need for any loop:

```
a$ = Ltrim$(a$)  'removes leading spaces from a$
```

Now that you have made sure that a$ does not start with a space, thus throwing your space and word counts off by one, what about double spaces after periods? Some typists still follow this practice.[5] Consider whether the routine counts the following correctly: "Hello. How are you?" (with two spaces after the period). How about "U.S.S. Enterprise"? (How many words does this string consist of, anyway?)

Covering all the possibilities is one of the most intellectually challenging aspects of writing computer applications.

Application 9 Team standings

Overview

The user enters six team names. When the user enters a number between 1 and 6, the program states which team is in that position (for example, that the Flyers are in position 1).

Learning Objectives

- making and using control arrays
- using the Edit menu's Copy and Paste commands
- setting initial conditions when the program begins
- changing text to a value
- monitoring the changing of a text box
- using Right$( )
- detecting the pressing of Enter
- moving the focus

Instructions

Figure 9-3 shows the application's form. Enter the title in a label box. Change its name to **Title**.

---

[5]The official rule for typists used to be to insert two spaces after a period. But that became a rule when typists were using typewriters, where each letter took up the same amount of room. You are reading a proportionally spaced font. An "i" is not as wide as a "w." When you are using proportional spacing, you leave only one space after the period.

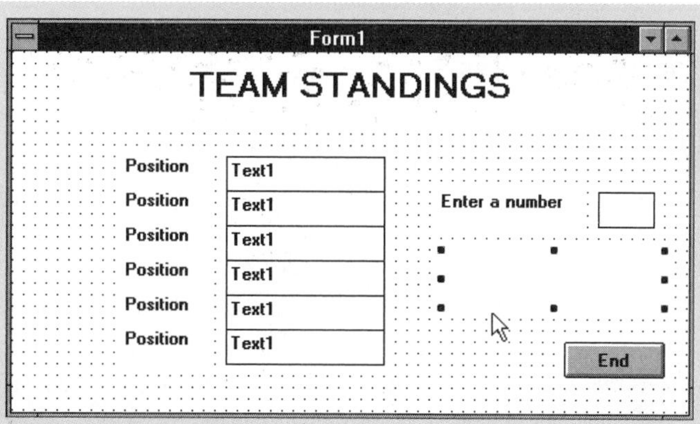

Figure 9-3
The Team Standings form at design time

For this application, you make two control arrays: six label boxes to hold the words Position 1, Position 2, and so on, and an array of six text boxes for the team names. Name your label boxes Position and your six text boxes TeamName.

First make your array of six text boxes. You can use the suggestion in Section 9.3 regarding matching the indices of the text boxes with the indices of the variable array. To do so, include in your form a text box in the position of the first Text1 box shown in Figure 9-3, *but one box-height higher*. (You delete this box later.) Change the text box's name to TeamName.

With this text box still selected, choose the Edit menu's Copy command. Although it seems as though nothing happens, the text box is on the computer's Clipboard and ready for pasting.

Open the Edit menu and choose Paste. You see the familiar Visual Basic dialog box warning that you are giving the new text box a name already in use. You are about to make an array of controls, so answer Yes. Visual Basic places a copy in the top-left corner of the form. The original is now `TeamName(0)` and the new one is `TeamName(1)`.

Move the new box underneath the first text box. Then choose the Edit menu's Paste command again. (You don't need to copy the text box again; a copy is still on the Clipboard.)

Keep pasting and moving until you have seven boxes in the form. Then select and delete the first text box. This leaves you with six text boxes, from `TeamName(1)` to `TeamName(6)`.

Now add a control array of six labels to the left of the six text boxes. After you place the first one, change both its name and caption to Position. Now go through the procedure of using the Edit menu's Copy and Paste commands to make five more Position boxes.

Here is another way to make their indices go from 1 to 6 rather than 0 to 5. Select the last Position label and click on Index in the properties list. If you followed the instructions in the last paragraph, this box, `Position(5)`, will have the index number of 5. Simply make its index 6. Click on the next box up and change its index from 4 to 5. Continue to the top.

Whichever way you do it, the final result should be six pairs of boxes: a Position(1) label followed by the TeamName(6) text box down to Position(6) and TeamName(6).

A common mistake is to end up with 12 boxes whose indices go from 1 to 12 or 0 to 11. This mistake occurs if you forget to change the control name and create text boxes rather than labels when you begin the second set of six boxes. You could change the incorrect names and index values, but it is faster to delete the boxes, make a new one with the correct name, and then copy and paste them again.

Another problem that can arise is for the index number to be out of order. Move the boxes, or simply change the numbers to put them in order from the top down.

Place on the form an empty text box called Number. To the right of the text box, add the label Enter with the message "Enter a number." Below this text box, add a larger label as shown in Figure 9-4. Call this label Info, and blank out its caption.

When the program runs, the form initially looks like Figure 9-4. While designing the form, you put the word Position in each box. As it runs, the program adds the digits after the word.

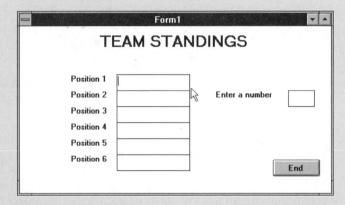

Figure 9-4
The form at run time, after loading

You could add these digits by "brute force," by clicking on each label and changing the name. However, there is a way to tell the program to do it automatically and empty the text boxes at the same time.

To begin execution, the program loads the first form. (Of course, this particular application has only one form.) One event of the form itself is Form_Load. Any code that you place in Form_Load gets executed when the form first appears, before control passes to the user. Double-click on the form itself (not on one of the controls). Form_Load's code window should appear. If not, select Object: Form and Proc: Load. Then add this code:

```
Sub Form_Load ()
   For i = 1 to 6
      Position(i).Caption = "Position" + Str$(i) 'add ⇒
      the number
      TeamName(i).text =""     ' quote-quote .... nothing
   Next i
   Number.text =""
End Sub
```

The Info box tells you the name of the team whose number is entered in the Number box. As always when programming in Visual Basic, you have to determine which action by the user is to trigger a response on the screen. In this case, you want the message in the Info box to change when the user changes the number in the Number box. Therefore, you put the following code into the event Number_Change:

```
Sub Number_Change ()
   If Number.text <> "" Then
      i = Val(Number.text)
      If i >= 1 And i <= 6 Then
         if TeamName(i).text <> "" Then
            if Right$(TeamName(i).text, 1) = "s" then
               a$=" are"
            else
               a$=" is"
            end if
            Info.Caption = TeamName(i).text + a$ + " in ⇒
               position " + Str$(i)
         End If
      Else
         Info.Caption = "No such team"
      End If
   Else
      Info.Caption = ""
   End If
End Sub
```

The preceding code demonstrates a good use of the **Right$** *function. In this case, you must check whether the team name is plural and include "are" or "is" in your message as appropriate.*

After coding your End button, run the application. Put team names into the text boxes, and a valid number into the other box. Is the message correct?

Modifications

1. The following improvement makes the program easier for the user. Usually you move from one box to the next by pressing Tab or clicking in a new area with the mouse. But many users are accustomed to pressing Enter after they finish an entry. To enable users to do so, add the following routine. Chapter 10 discusses this routine in detail, but try using it to enhance this application.

Double-click on a TeamName object and pick **KeyDown** from the action **(Proc)** list. (Alternatively, you can simply open the code window and start typing.)

```
Sub TeamName_KeyDown (index As Integer, keycode As
   Integer, Shift As ⇒ Integer)
   If keycode = 13 Then      'ENTER was pressed
      index = index + 1: If index = 7 Then index = 1 ⇒
         'wrap around bottom to top
      TeamName(index).SetFocus 'give the focus to the ⇒
         next index
   End If
End Sub
```

2. Suppose that the upper-right text box displays a message such as "Detroit is in position 1." If the user changes the team name's spelling, will the program update the message box? Decide the event in which to place the code to correct this oversight and then add the code.

Enhancement

Suppose once again that the application displays the message "Detroit is in position 1." The program would be better if it announced "Detroit is in first place" (or, if you are not from Detroit, maybe "Detroit is in last place"!). Change the program to say "first," "second," "third," and so on.

In **Sub Number_Change**, you could use a **Select Case** statement that covers all the possibilities. However, a more elegant way is to define another array to hold these words in general declarations:

```
Dim word$(6)
```

Then define words in Form_Load and use the word$( ) array to compose your comment. For example, TeamName(i) in Position(i) will use word$(i). You can define your words in Sub Form_Load:

```
Sub Form_Load
   word$(1) = "first"
   word$(2) = "second"
   ... and so on.
```

Exercises

At your desk

1. What will num(5) contain after you run the following routines?

a.
```
Dim num(10)
For i = 1 To 10
   num(i) = i * 3
Next i
```

b.
```
Dim num(5)
For i= 1 To 5
    num(i) = num(i - 1)+ i
Next i
```

2. Suppose that you have a control array of check boxes called CB. Your properties list shows that you are dealing with CB(4). What is the index of this check box?

3. What appears in Label1 if the following code sets the label's caption?

```
Label1.Caption = "A"+ Chr$(32) + "B"
```

4. After you copy Label1 and paste its copy in the form, what message appears? What will be the name of the new control if you answer Yes? What will be the name if you answer No?

5. *By default*, what is the index of the first control in a control array?

6. If a$ = "THEREFORE", what are the contents of abc.Caption if

a. `abc.Caption = Left$(a$, 5)`
b. `abc.Caption = Right$(a$, 4)`
c. `abc.Caption = Mid$(a$, 7, 2)`
d. `abc.Caption = Str$(Len(a$))`

7. What is the purpose of a **Dim** statement? Where in the code do you place it?

At your computer

Create the application shown in Figure 9-5. The user simply clicks an option button and the correct message appears.

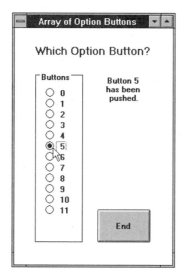

Figure 9-5
An application with an array of option buttons

The application requires just five lines of code: one to produce the message, one for the End button, and three to number the option buttons automatically. (You could set each button's caption yourself manually, but the three lines are faster and work just as well for 20 buttons.) Remember to place the frame before creating any option buttons.

Caution: After pasting each option button, click the frame to make sure that the next option button goes into the frame. Move the frame occasionally to ensure that your buttons are actually attached to the frame instead of just sitting on top of the frame (and thus only seems to be in the correct position).

Programming Adventure 1
Cash Register and Invoice Maker

This programming adventure involves more than one form. You make a simplified version of a real-life application: a cash register program that creates an invoice.

PA1.1 Using more than one form

Traditional non-Windows programs often begin with an introductory screen before displaying the main application screen. Your Visual Basic applications can have this feature also. You can do this by creating programs that use more than one form. While showing your first form on the screen, you can open a new form on top of the first one, or hide Form1 and show the second form.

Showing and hiding the second form

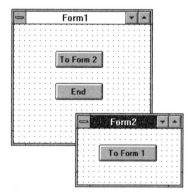

Figure PA1-1
Two forms

To see how to use multiple forms, try this short activity. First make a form with two buttons. Then open the File menu and choose New Form. Place a button on this new form. Your screen should now look similar to Figure PA1-1.

Your project window now lists two forms. Switch back and forth between the forms by selecting them from the project window or, if you can see them, by clicking on them. Resizing each form makes working with them more convenient.

Enter the following code for the two buttons on Form1. The **Sub** names show you what the buttons are called.

```
Sub ToForm2_Click ()
  Form2.Show
End Sub

Sub EndButton_Click ()
  End
End Sub
```

The following is the code for the button on Form2:

```
Sub ToForm1_Click
  Form2.Hide
End Sub
```

If you run the application and press the **To Form 2** button, you see the second form. However, you will notice, if you can see them, that Form1's buttons are still active. You can still end the program by clicking on the Form1's **End** button while Form2 is visible.

Modal forms

To make Form2 take complete control and disable Form1's buttons, make this change:

```
Sub ToForm2_CLick ()
  Form2.SHow 1
End Sub
```

Using the "1" makes Form2 now a *modal* form. Similar to a message box (**MsgBox**), the second form must be closed before events on any other forms are allowed.

If, instead of popping Form2 up on top of Form1, you wish to close the first form first, then modify **Sub** ToForm2_Click:

```
Sub ToForm2_Click ()
  Form1.Hide
  Form2.Show 1
  Form1.Show
End Sub
```

The above code illustrates an important concept to understand. The program transfers control from Form1 to Form2 during the ToForm2_Click event (i.e. before this **Sub** had ended.) When the program returns to Form1, execution continues where it left off. Check this out by adding **Stop**s in these places:

```
Sub ToForm2_Click ()
  Form1.Hide
  Stop
```

```
        Form2.Show 1
        Stop
        Form1.Show
    End Sub
```

Run the program once again, click the To Form 2 button. The program breaks at the first **Stop**. Press F5 to continue: Form2 appears. Press Form2's button, and the program breaks at the second **Stop**. It is important to realize that **Sub**s run to completion unless they are interrupted. Transferring control to a modal form causes such an interruption. As a last experiment, remove the **Stop**s from ToForm2_Click and remove the 1 from the **Show** line:

```
    Sub ToForm2_Click ()
        Form1.Hide
        Form2.Show    'modeless form (not a modal form)
        Form1.Show
    End Sub
```

If you don't create Form2 as a modal form and Form1 is larger than Form2, you might never see the second form when you press the **To Form 2** button. Remember this while working on multiple form applications.

Sharing variables between forms

When you dimension a variable in a form's general declarations, that variable becomes global throughout that form only. All **Sub**s will know the value of the variable. However, the variable will not be common to the other forms in your application.

Just as **Sub** procedures make up a form, forms are grouped in a *module*. To enable two forms to share a variable, you create a module and declare the variable to be **global** in the module's general declarations section.

To make a module that contains the two forms that you created in the preceding section, open the File menu and choose New Module. You see Module1.bas, the default name, on your project list.

In the module's general declarations, type the following:

```
    Global num As Integer.
```

This makes num a common variable in the entire application. To show that both forms know the value of num, add a line to each of the forms' Form_Paint (not Form_Load) procedures:

```
    Print num
```

When you run your program, you should see zeros in the top-left corner of each form. Of course, that doesn't prove that the two forms are sharing the value of num. You must give num a nonzero value. One method is to assign a value to num in Form1's **Sub** Form_Load procedure. This method assumes that Form1 will be the first form that appears in your application, which is the default situation. Add the following line to Form1's Form_Load routine:

```
num = 5
```

Then run your program.

Using a Sub Main Procedure

A cleaner method of assigning values to variables in a multiform application is to use a special subprocedure, **Sub Main**, in your module. To do this, switch to the module's code window. (Choose Module1.bas from your project window.) Then type **Sub Main** in the general declarations (just as you create any new named Sub procedure). Assign num a value in those declarations:[1]

```
Sub Main ()        'in Module1's code window
   num = 10
   form1.show        'start with form1
End Sub
```

Now open the Options menu, choose the Project command, and select Start Up Form. You then see the Setting drop-down list shown in Figure PA1-2. This list is where you specify the form that you want your application to run first when it starts. Select **Sub Main** from the drop-down list.

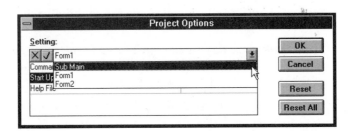

Figure PA1-2
Start with Sub Main in the module or with one of the forms

Before running your program, make sure that you remove the num = 5 line from Form1.Load.

In the preceding example, you used the command **Print** to place text directly on the form rather than in a label or text box. The next section deals with printing on the form.

---

[1] In multiple form applications, assign initial values to global variables in Sub Main rather than in the Form_Load (or other) procedures in the various forms composing your application. This saves you from later having to hunt through a lot of code trying to find out where num got its initial value.

PA1.2   Printing and drawing lines on a form

In this application, you bring up a form that displays a printed table inside some grid lines. Try this simple example to learn the necessary techniques.

Drawing lines

Place and code an End button on a blank Form1. Then code these two **Sub**s:

```
Sub Form_Load ()
  ScaleHeight = 1000
  ScaleWidth = 1000
End Sub

Sub Form_Paint ()
  Line (100, 150)-(900, 150), 0
  Line (100, 160)-(900, 160), 0
  Line (100, 100)-(900, 800), 0, B
End Sub
```

The ScaleHeight and ScaleWidth commands set a scale for your form. Your form's actual height and width across the screen doesn't matter; after the form's ScaleHeight is set, your form will be considered to be 1,000 units high. Do not confuse Form1's ScaleHeight with its actual Height. The form's height remains at whatever you set it when you designed the form. But for graphical purposes, you can consider the form to go from (0,0) in the top-left corner to (1000,1000) in the bottom-right corner.

After the form loads, the program "paints" the controls on the form as shown in Figure PA1.3. In Form_Paint, you told the program to draw two figures. The first is a line. The syntax for drawing the line is as follows:

```
Line (x1, y1) - (x2, y2), color
```

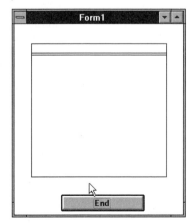

Figure PA1-3
Lines drawn at run time

Adding a ", B" at the end of the line statement creates a box. The code first drew the two middle horizontal lines and then the box around the outside. (Can you see how you could draw the two middle lines using one Line statement?)

Printing text on the form

So far, you have displayed text on the screen by placing captions in labels. You can **print** the text directly to the form (or to any control) after setting the x and y position for the text with **CurrentX**, **CurrentY**. Modify your Form_Paint routine as follows:

```
Sub Form_Paint ()
  Line (100, 150)-(900, 150), 0
  Line (100, 160)-(900, 160), 0
  Line (100, 100)-(900, 800), 0, B

  CurrentX = 340: CurrentY = 100 'set the coordinates
  Print "Sample Table"

  For y = 200 To 500 Step 50     'count by 50's from ⇒
    200 to 500
    CurrentX = 230
    CurrentY = y
    Print "This is CurrentY = "; y
  Next y

End Sub
```

*This code demonstrates a **For...Next** loop that doesn't count by 1, which is the default increment if you omit the **Step** value. But you can count by other values:*

```
For i = 10 To 1 Step -1 'count backward
Next i

For i = 1 To 9 Step 2    'odd number between 1 to 9 ⇒
  (inclusive)
Next i

For i = -1 To + 1 Step .05 'small increments
Next i
```

In Figure PA1-4 you can see how the printing appeared on the form, as positioned with the CurrentX and CurrentY statements.

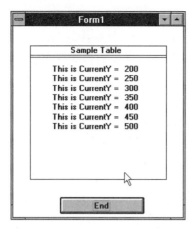

Figure PA1-4
Lines and printing on the form

Application PA1 Cash register and invoice maker

Overview

The user selects items from a pulldown menu and adds them to the list of items purchased. By clicking on a button, the user obtains an invoice for the sale. For each item selected, the application displays the item's quantity, price, and name.

Learning Objectives

- using more than one form
- printing and drawing on a form
- scaling a form
- making a form's size unchangeable
- using named subprocedures
- formatting numbers
- working with different fonts
- using KeyDown to check for the Enter key
- adjusting the TabIndex of a form's controls
- performing an action when controls get the focus

Instructions

For this application, you make two forms and a global module. In the global module, you define the variables that you need to be common to the two forms.

Open the File menu and choose New Module.[2] If you don't see a code window for the module, highlight the module name in the project window and click the View Code button. In the module's general declarations, declare the following variables to be global:

```
Global itemcost(20) As Single
Global itemname$(20)
Global quantity(20) As Integer
Global items As Integer
```

Three of the preceding lines are arrays with 20 as the highest allowed index. Some of the variables are defined as **Integer**, some as **Single**-precision decimal variables, and one as a string.

Form1 contains eight labels, including the title (see Figure PA1-5). All have centered captions (select Alignment and choose the option 2-Center).

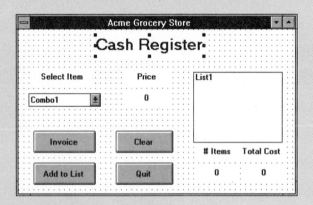

Figure PA1-5
Form1

This is a good time to use the Edit menu's Copy and Paste commands to save you from having to set all the alignments one at a time. Three of the labels have a zero as their caption, so use one of those as your pattern.

The control names that you use for the labels that represent the form's headings really don't matter. But change the control names of the labels with the zeros as follows:

Control	Control's location
Itemprice	(label underneath the **Price** label)
number	(below # **Items**)
Total	(Below **Total Cost**)

The form has a combo box and a list box. (Be careful that you don't use the text box or frame control in place of the list box control.) You preload the combo box

---

[2]In Visual Basic 1, the module is called Global.bas, and is automatically created when you begin a new application.

with items and store each item's price in the program. The prices reside in an array, `cost( )`. Many procedures in the form use these figures, so dimension the array in general declarations:

```
Dim cost(5)
```

This code line makes `cost()` a global variable in Form1 *but not in Form2*, the second form that you create for this two-form application. That's why you are declaring it in Form1, not in Module1.

The combo box hold items that you can purchase. To stock the box and set each item's price, place this code in Form_Load:

```
Sub Form_Load ()
   Combo1.AddItem "Bread": cost(0) = 1.58
   Combo1.AddItem "Milk": cost(1) = 1.99
   Combo1.AddItem "Butter": cost(2) = 2.5
   Combo1.AddItem "Orange Juice": cost(3) = 1
End Sub
```

(You reserved room for two more costs, so add two others if you want. Choose something under $1 to see how the program displays the price.)

When the user clicks on an item in the combo box, it displays the item's price in the Itemprice label. Add the following code to the combo box:

```
Sub Combo1_Click ()
   Itemprice.Caption = Format$(cost(Combo1.Listindex),⇨
     "##0.00")
End Sub
```

To add this item to the shopping list, the user clicks on the Add to List button. The computer keeps track of the item's name and price. Later the program displays an invoice showing the ordered items. But if the user clicks on Bread twice, the program should detect that the user is not selecting a new item and should instead increase the quantity and total cost of the bread ordered. Create the Add to List button and enter this code:

```
Sub AddButton_Click ()
  If Combo1.ListIndex >= 0 Then            'if there are items on the list
    chosen$ = Combo1.Text                  'the one in the box
    list1.AddItem chosen$                  'add this one to the list
    number.Caption = Str$(list1.ListCount) 'update number count
    x = Val(Total.Caption) ⇒
      + cost(Combo1.ListIndex)             'add to total price
    Total.Caption = Format$(x, "###.00")   'display total price

'see if the item to be added (chosen$) is a new
                                'category or more of a previous category
    newone = 1                  'assume item is a new one for now
    For i = 1 To items          'for each item on the shopping list ...
```

```
    If itemname$(i) = chosen$        'if it's the one added
      quantity(i) = quantity(i) + 1  'update that one's quantity
      newone = 0                     'not a new one after all
      i = items
    End If
  Next i
  If newone = 1 Then                           'there was a change in the invoice
     items = items + 1                          'another item category is created
     quantity(items) = 1                        'there is one item in this new ⇒
                                                  category
     itemcost(items) = cost(Combo1.ListIndex)  'cost of this item
     itemname$(items) = chosen$                'name for this item category
   End If
  End If
End Sub
```

Make one last adjustment: find Combo1's Style property and set it to 2 (the drop-down list).

Run the program and select some items. Figure PA1-6 shows that the user is just about to add orange juice to the shopping list.

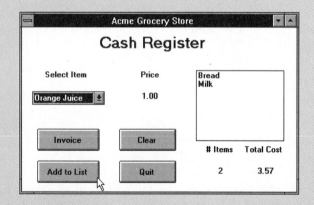

Figure PA1-6
The shopping list application in action

The second form that you create will be called Invoice. Clicking on Form1's InvoiceButton will cause the new form to be displayed (see Figure PA1-6).

```
Sub InvoiceButton_Click ()
    Invoice.Show 1
End Sub
```

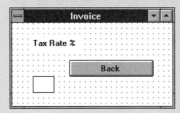

```
┌──────────────────────────────────────────┐
│ ─                Invoice                  │
│            Acme Grocery Store             │
│                                           │
│  ┌─────────────┬──────┬──────┬──────┐    │
│  │ Item        │Quant │ Unit │ Cost │    │
│  │             │      │      │      │    │
│  │  Bread      │  1   │ 1.58 │ 1.58 │    │
│  │  Milk       │  2   │ 1.99 │ 3.98 │    │
│  │  Orange Juice│ 1   │ 1.00 │ 1.00 │    │
│  │             │      │      │      │    │
│  │             │      │      │      │    │
│  │             ├──────┴──────┼──────┤    │
│  │             │    Subtotal │ 6.56 │    │
│  │ Tax Rate %  │        Tax  │ 0.49 │    │
│  │    [7.5]    │      Total  │ 7.05 │    │
│  │  ┌────────────────────┐   │           │
│  │  │       Back         │   │           │
│  │  └────────────────────┘   │           │
│  └───────────────────────────┘           │
└──────────────────────────────────────────┘
```

Figure PA1-7
The invoice form at run time

Now create your second form, as shown in Figure PA1.8. Open the File menu and choose New Form. Make the form's name Invoice. Call the label TaxLabel, the text box TaxBox, and the button BackButton.

```
┌──────────────────────────────────┐
│ ─        Invoice         ▼ ▲      │
│ Tax Rate %                        │
│          ┌──────────────┐         │
│          │     Back     │         │
│          └──────────────┘         │
│   ┌────┐                          │
│   │    │                          │
│   └────┘                          │
└──────────────────────────────────┘
```

Figure PA1-8
The second form at design time

The size that you make the form or the controls doesn't matter, because each is set in Form_Load. Also, to prevent the user from altering the size of the form, make the form size unchangeable by setting the form's BorderStyle to 3 (fixed double).

Here are Invoice's general declarations:

```
Dim taxrate as single
```

Now enter the following in Form_Load:

```
Sub Form_Load ()
  taxrate = .075
  Invoice.Left = 1425: Invoice.Top = 975
  Invoice.Width = 7425: Invoice.Height  = 5910
```

```
            Taxbox.Width = 600: Taxbox.Height = 375
            Taxbox.Left = 1900: Taxbox.Top = 4200
            Taxbox.Text = Format$(taxrate * 100, "##0.##")

            TaxLabel.Left = 720: TaxLabel.Top = 4250
            TaxLabel.Width = 1095: TaxLabel.Height = 275
            TaxLabel.Caption = "Tax Rate %"

            BackButton.Left = 730: BackButton.Top = 4800
            BackButton.Width = 2980: BackButton.Height = 375

        End Sub
```

You need two general **Sub** procedures. The first is DrawInvoice, which scales the form, sets controls in the correct places, draws a grid, and prints headings:

```
Sub DrawInvoice ()
    Cls                'clear the form's screen
    'set scaling parameters to make calculations easier
    ScaleLeft = 0: ScaleTop = 0
    ScaleHeight = 1000: ScaleWidth = 1000

    'print the headings
    CurrentX = 340: CurrentY = 20 'cursor location for ⇒
        title
    Print "Acme Grocery Store"
    CurrentX = 110: CurrentY = 155
    Print "Item";            'semicolon leaves cursor
    CurrentX = 506           ' on same line, so CurrentY
    Print "Quant";           ' need not be repeated.
    CurrentX = 640: Print "Unit";
    CurrentX = 790: Print "Cost "
    CurrentY = 710
    CurrentX = 590: Print "Subtotal"
    CurrentX = 676: CurrentY = 760: Print "Tax"
    CurrentY = 816
    CurrentX = 644: Print "Total"

    'draw the grid
    Line (100, 150)-(900, 700), 0, B
    Line (100, 200)-(900, 200), 0
    Line (750, 150)-(900, 860), 0, B
    Line (500, 150)-(600, 700), 0, B
    Line (640, 800)-(900, 800)

End Sub
```

Note that the preceding routine, which executes after Form_Load, sets scaling factors. For that reason, Form_Load specifies the sizes and positions of the form's controls in absolute numbers. Alternatively, you could draw the button, text box, and label in DrawInvoice. In that case, you would specify positions and sizes as a fraction of 1,000.

The second general **Sub** is ProcessInvoice, which does some calculations and fits the results into the appropriate locations on the invoice:

```
Sub processinvoice ()
  fontname = "Courier" 'screen.fonts(0)
  subtotal = 0
  For i = 1 To items                 'for each separate item
    CurrentX = 150
    'each line will be 30 below the previous line
    CurrentY = 250 + i * 30
    Print itemname$(i);
    a$ = Format$(quantity(i), "##")
    s$ = Space$(8)
    'put a$ in the right side of s$
    RSet s$ = a$

    CurrentX = 420
    Print s$;

    a$ = Format$(itemcost(i), "##0.00")
    s$ = Space$(8)
    RSet s$ = a$
    CurrentX = 588
    Print s$;

    t = quantity(i) * itemcost(i) 'cost of that many ⇒
      items
    a$ = Format$(t, "####0.00")
    s$ = Space$(8)
    RSet s$ = a$
    CurrentX = 724
    Print s$

    subtotal = subtotal + t          'keep a running ⇒
      subtotal
  Next i

  x = 724
  CurrentX = x
  CurrentY = 710
  a$ = Format$(subtotal, "###0.00"")
  s$ = Space$(8)
  RSet s$ = a$
  Print s$
```

```
      fillstyle = 0

      Line (780, 760)-(890, 790), QBColor(15), BF ⇒
        'white box

      CurrentX = x: CurrentY = 760
      tax = subtotal * taxrate
      a$ = Format$(tax, "###0.00")
      s$ = Space$(8)
      RSet s$ = a$                          'the tax
      Print s$

      Line (780, 810)-(890, 850), QBColor(15), BF
      CurrentX = x: CurrentY = 816
      a$ = Format$(subtotal + tax, "###0.00")
      s$ = Space$(8)
      RSet s$ = a$
      Print s$                              'grand total
      fillstyle = 1 'back to transparent boxes (the ⇒
        default value)
   End Sub
```

In all columns of numbers, you should align decimal points. This is quite tricky because common fonts have proportional spacing–a "1" takes less space than an "8". For that reason, you change the font to Courier, an equal-spacing font. Alternatively, you could use Monospaced as well.

If you look up **Format$** in the Help screens, you find that you can automatically display a dollar sign. Unfortunately, this leads to problems because the value of a label with a leading dollar sign is always zero.

The **RSet** function places one string inside another at the right end. So if the string s$ consists of eight spaces, RSet s$ = a$ places a$ in the right side of s$. That is, enough leading characters are added to make a$ eight spaces long. This enables you to align decimal points.

Windows is a graphical environment. When you print text to the screen, Windows doesn't replace one character with another, but instead draws letters over anything else on the screen. Thus previous printing shows through the new characters. This is a potential problem for regions on the invoice that change, such as the tax and total areas that update when the user alters the tax rate. The ProcessInvoice code uses Line statements with the BF (box filled) option to place filled, white boxes over any previous values before printing a new values in their place:

```
   Line (x1, y1) - (x2, y2) , color, BF
```

QBColor(15) is white. However, by default, filled boxes are transparent, so you can place a color over of some text for highlighting purposes. To make the box opaque, you set FillStyle to 1.

At the bottom left of the form is a value for the tax calculation. You want to enable the user to change the tax rate. You could calculate a new tax total every time the user presses a key while entering a new rate. This event would be Taxbox_Change. Instead, you could update the invoice when the user finishes changing the Tax figure. But how do you know when the user is done? You could demand that the user press Enter, and watch for that event.

But an interesting technique is to watch for the user to click on or tab to the Taxbox. This triggers the GotFocus event, which tells you that that the user is about to alter the tax rate. You can wipe the old value, change the caption of BackButton to "Update," and wait for the user either to press Enter or click on the "recaptioned" BackButton:

```
Sub Taxbox_GotFocus ()
    Taxbox.Text = ""
    BackButton.Caption = "Update"
End Sub
```

If no value is in the Taxbox when the user presses Enter, restore the old value. Alternatively, use the new value and recalculate the totals on the invoice. Return BackButton to its original caption:

```
Sub Taxbox_KeyDown (keycode As Integer, Shift As ⇒
   Integer)
  If keycode = 13 Then         'Enter pressed
    If Taxbox.Text = "" Then  'nothing there
        Taxbox.Text = Format$(taxrate * 100, "##0.##") ⇒
          'restore it
    Else
        taxrate = Val(Taxbox.Text) / 100  'new value
        processinvoice                    'recalculate
    End If
    BackButton.SetFocus
    BackButton.CapTion = "Back"
  End If
End Sub
```

Taxbox would lose the focus if the user clicked elsewhere. In that case, if the box is empty return it to its old value:

```
Sub Taxbox_LostFocus ()
        If Taxbox.Text = "" Then Taxbox.Text = ⇒
          Format$(taxrate * 100, "##0.##")
End Sub
```

Finally, deal with the clicking of the BackButton. If the button's caption is Update, calculate new totals from the new tax rate, if one has been entered. If BackButton's caption is Back, return to Form1 by hiding Form2:

```
Sub BackButton_Click ()
    If BackButton.Caption = "Update" Then
      BackButton.Caption = "Back"  'switch the ⇒
        caption back
```

```
                      If Taxbox.Text <> "" Then      'something has been
                         typed
                         taxrate = Val(Taxbox.Text) / 100   'new value
                         processinvoice                  'recalculate
                      End If
                   Else
                      Invoice.Hide          'back to form1
                   End If
```

Finally, remember that if you return to the invoice, Invoice has already been loaded. (It's just hiding.) You must redraw the invoice:

```
Sub Form_Paint ()
    drawinvoice
    processinvoice
End Sub
```

Modifications

1. If you know how to use **For...Next** loops, you can add a button to remove al the items from the list box and set the numbers back to zero. To find an example in the Help screens, search for **remove item** (go to **RemoveItem method**).

2. See whether you can make a routine that enables the user to add items to a style zero combo box. You can put the routine in Combo1_Change or AddButton_Click. In the AddButton code, you would include an **Else** followed by the appropriate code, because if Combo1.Listindex is not >= 0, the user's item is not on the list. How will you get the new item's cost? You might use an **InputBox** and code similar to the following:

```
newnum = Combo1.Listcount + 1
Cost(newnum) = Val(InputBox$("How much does "+ ⇒
  Combo1.Text + " cost?"))
```

You can use **Combo1.AddItem** to put the new item on the list.

3. How many items can you add before getting an error? How can you guard against adding an item after you reach the limit that you set in the program's Declarations section? (You know how large an array you can have because you dimensioned your arrays in the Declarations section. But you also can use a **Ubound** function to find this limit. Look up **arrays** in the Help screens to find out how to determine the boundaries of an array.)

4. You printed the company name. You might instead define a label for it, and use a text box on the first form to accept the company name. That would make the program more flexible.

Enhancement

You might have noticed that the first form has a Clear button. The user clicks on this button to clear the list box. Try to code the button. You must blank out any itemname$( )'s that you have filled, reduce items to zero, and clear the item-cost( ) and quantity( ) arrays.

Chapter 10 Manipulating Data

All but your simplest Visual Basic applications will request much data from the user, such as names and addresses, stock figures, or book titles. A well-designed *input form* enables the user to enter the data easily. In this chapter, you learn techniques for creating user-friendly forms designed to accept and display many data items.

When dealing with large amounts of data, you usually use arrays. After processing the data, you often display the information in a numerical, alphabetical, or chronological order. To do so, you need *sort routines*.

10.1 Sorting numbers and words

Visual Basic knows, of course, that two is greater than one. If number(1) contains the value 27 and number(2) equals 10, Visual Basic knows that number(1) is greater than number(2). This gives you the capability to sort an array of numbers in numerical order.

Visual Basic also ranks letter: B is greater than A, ZEBRA is greater than ELEPHANT, APPLE is greater than APE. Thus you can sort arrays containing strings of alphanumeric characters (such as words) in alphabetical order. But you must provide the code to do so.

There are several different sorting algorithms. The shortest, Bubble Sort, happens to be the slowest, but is also the easiest to understand. Let's try tracking it. (To use Bubble Sort, you need not understand how it works; you can simply code the code. However, it's worth trying to follow the procedure, just for the fun of it!)

Suppose that you have four playing cards lined up in front of you, in random order, as shown in Figure 10-1. You want to put them in order. How do you do this?

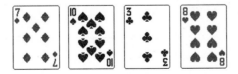

Figure 10-1
Four cards to be sorted

This is one case where doing the task is easier than describing *how* you do it. If asked, you would probably say that you simply pick up the card with the lowest number and put it first. But how do you determine which is the lowest letter? By doing a series of comparisons.

Try this system. Start by taking the first card in your left hand and the second in your right (Figure 10-2).

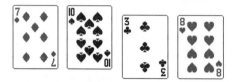

Figure 10-2
Compare the first two cards

If the first card is larger, exchange the cards between your hands. This moves the lower of the two cards to your left hand. Whether you swap the cards or not, put down the card in your right hand and pick up the next one (Figure 10-3).

Figure 10-3
Compare the first and third cards

Again compare the two cards and swap them if the right hand holds a lower card (Figure 10-4).

Figure 10-4
Swap the two cards

Continue until your right hand reaches the end of the line, switching cards in each hand if necessary. At the end of the first pass, your left hand is holding the lowest card. (Figure 10.5)

Figure 10-5
Compare first and fourth cards

Put this lowest card down and move your left hand one card to the right. Pick up card two in your left hand and card three in your right (Figure 10-6) and repeat the process. Each time that your right hand finishes with the last card in the line, your left hand will be holding the next lowest card.

Figure 10-6
Compare the second and third cards

Finally, you pick up the second-to-last card in your left hand and the last in your right. Either you swap them or you don't. Then you put them down. You are finished; the set of cards is sorted.

Here is the Visual Basic code for this operation. Imagine that the card values are in an array called Card( ). Thus Card(1) = 7, Card(2) = 10, Card(3) = 3, and so on, up to Card(n) where n is the number of different cards. In this case, n = 4, so Card(n), the last card, is 8. L represents your left hand and R your right hand. Here is Bubble Sort's code:

```
For L = 1 To n-1     'left hand will pick up card 1, then 2, then 3
   For R = L+1 To n  'right starts at next card and goes to last card
      If Letter$(L) > Letter$(R) Then      'if left card > right card
         temp$ = Letter$(L)                'save left card
         Letter$(L) = Letter$(R)           'put right card into left "hand"
         Letter(R) = temp$                 'pick up saved (left) card in right
      End If
   Next R
Next L
```

Again, the Bubble Sort is not a fast sort for large value of n, but is the easiest to understand.

10.2 Reacting to key presses

In Application 9, the user enters team names in successive text boxes. The standard keyboard method that Windows allows for moving from one box to another is by pressing the Tab key. But many users, seeing a vertical list, expect that pressing Enter after making an entry will cause the cursor to move to the next box. Also, to many users, it is intuitive that the cursor up and down arrow keys move the cursor up and down a series of text boxes.

In the modifications to Application 8, you were invited to check for the pressing of Enter and change the focus as if the user pressed Tab. This section presents more detailed information about this process.

Learning by reading works, but learning by doing works better. The best way to study how to detect key presses is to experiment. Create the small application shown in Figure 10-7.

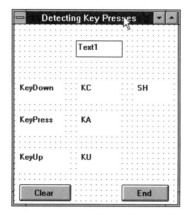

Figure 10-7
The form for a small application that detects key presses

The form includes a text box, three descriptive labels, and four labels on the right with names KC, SH, KP, and KU.

Code your two buttons and then enter the following instructions into Text1's KeyDown, KeyPress, and KeyUp routines:

```
Sub Text1_KeyDown (KeyCode As Integer, Shift As Integer)
  KC.Caption = "Keycode: " + Str$(KeyCode)
  SH.Caption = "Shift: " + Str$(Shift)
End Sub

Sub Text1_KeyPress (KeyAscii As Integer)
  KA.Caption = "KeyAscii" + Str$(KeyAscii)
End Sub

Sub Text1_KeyUp (KeyCode As Integer, Shift As Integer)
  KU.Caption = "KeyCode " + Str$(KeyCode)
  SH.Caption = "Shift: " + Str$(Shift)
End Sub
```

Run this experimentation program and press some keys. Try holding keys down. Try Shift, the cursor arrow keys, or Backspace. What happens when you release a key?

When you press and release a key while in Text1 (that is, while Text1 *has the focus*), all three events take place. Find out the order in which they execute by putting **Stop** before the **End Sub** in each and seeing where the program stops. Open the Run menu, choose Continue, and see what happens.

In Application 10, you use the up and down arrow keys and the Tab and Enter keys. Find out their KeyAscii and KeyCode values.

Application 10   **Sorting Swords**

This important application shows you how to have the computer create text boxes at run time, sort a list of words, and react to the pressing of the Enter and cursor arrow keys. Figure 10-8 shows the application's form at run time.

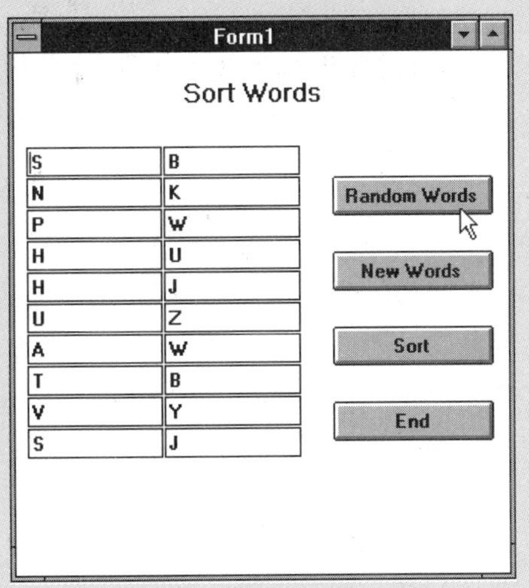

Figure 10-8
The form for Application 10 at run time

Overview

The user can enter as many as 12 words and have them sorted in alphabetical order. To move up and down a list, you use the cursor movement keys.

Learning Objectives

- making an array of text boxes using Copy and Paste
- defining an array
- creating objects at run time
- sorting an array
- monitoring and processing key presses
- coding the cursor movement keys
- using **Space$** and **Len**

Instructions

Although at run time the form has 20 text boxes, you need to create only one. You will then write some code in Form_Load to make the rest of them. As the program runs, the other nineteen boxes will appear.

Figure 10-9 shows all the controls you have to add during the design process. Call your single text box **Word**. When the program starts, it will automatically remove the caption Text1. Set the Index property to 0. This setting tells the computer that the Word text box is part of a control array.

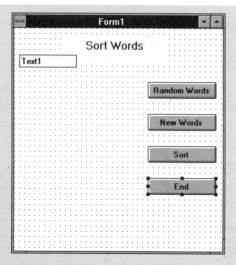

Figure 10-9
The finished form

Make the four buttons and name them Random, New, Sort, and End.

Here is the logic of Form_Load. First the program creates boxes 1 to 10. The statement that creates these boxes is Load Word(i). Each box has the same left side as box Word(0). The top of Word(0) is Word(0).Top. The top of Word(1) is Word(0).Top plus Word(0).Height plus a little extra to separate the boxes. So in general, the top of Word(i) is Word(i - 1).Top plus Word(i - 1).Height plus the spacing amount.

The program creates Word(11) to Word(20) similarly. These boxes' tops are the tops of those beside them, and the boxes' left sides are the left sides of the adjacent box plus its width plus a number for the space between columns.

After loading a new control, the program has to make it visible.

At the end of Form_Load, you set each control's *TabIndex* property. This setting ensures that the focus moves from word to word in sequence, starting with Word(1).

Finally, you place random characters into the boxes. The actual coding for generating the random characters takes place in the **Sub** Random_Click. As you enter the following code, you'll notice that you can cause the same thing to happen in Form_Load with the simple one line instruction Call Random_Click. Here is Form_Load:

```
Sub Form_Load ()
    'You already have a Word(0) box
    'create Word(1) to Word(10)
  For i = 1 To 10
    Load Word(i) 'create a another "Word" box
    Word(i).Left = Word(0).Left 'same as your pattern box
    Word(i).Top = Word(i - 1).Top + Word(0).Height + 15 ⇒
    'farther down
    Word(i).Visible = True        'show it
```

```
  Next i
     'create Word(11) to Word(20)
  For i = 11 To 20
     Load Word(i)
     besideit = i - 10    'i value in first column
     Word(i).Left = Word(besideit).Left + Word(besideit).Width + 20
     Word(i).Visible = True
     Word(i).Top = Word(besideit).Top
  Next i


  For i = 1 To 20        'set TabIndexes (ahead of  buttons)
     Word(i).TabIndex = i
  Next i


  Word(0).Visible = False  'hide your pattern Word(0) box


  Call Random_Click       'execute Code random button's code

End Sub
```

The following is the code for the Sort button:

```
Sub Sort_Click ()

For i = 1 To 19                    '"left hand" picks up a card
  For j = i + 1 To 20              ' right hand's card

    If UCase$(Word(i)) > UCase$(Word(j)) Then   'swap them
      temp$ = Word(i).Text
      Word(i).Text = Word(j).Text
      Word(j).Text = temp$
    End If

  Next j
Next i
                'look for blank words and bubble up any
                'below to take their places
For i = 1 To 19
  temp$ = Word(i).Text
  If temp$ = "" Or temp$ = Space$(Len(temp$)) Then
    For j = i + 1 To 20
      Word(j - 1).Text = Word(j).Text      'move each up one
    Next j
    Word(20).Text = "" 'blank the last one
    i = i - 1   'try it again for this i before moving on
  End If

Next i
Word(1).SetFocus    'put cursor in first word box
End Sub
```

The preceding code sorts the Word text boxes themselves. Alternatively, you could have dimensioned an array and then copied the 20 instances of Word( ).Text into the array. You could then have sorted the array and copied the array back into the boxes. A reason for using a variable array is to help you do many other tasks with the words, such as searching through the list for a match. However, this application does not use a variable array. By sorting the text boxes rather than a variable array, you actually get to see the sort take place on the screen.

Recall that every character has a corresponding ASCII value. The uppercase alphabet goes from 65 to 90 (that is, an A is **Chr$**(65) and, conversely, **ASC**("A") is 65). The Random_Click code uses Visual Basic's **Rnd** function to assign a character to each text box. **Rnd** results in a number between 0 and 1. You need 26 possible numbers (for the letters), so you multiply by 26 (producing numbers between 0 and 25.99999). By adding 65, the random numbers go between 65 and 90.99999. By using the Int function, you get integers between 65 and 90. Here is Random_Click's code:

```
Sub Random_Click ()
  For i = 1 To 20
    Word(i).Text = Chr$(Int(Rnd * 26) + 65)
  Next i
End Sub
```

The New button must erase all the Word(i).Texts, where i goes from 1 to 20:

```
Sub New_Click ()
For i = 1 To 20
 Word(i).Text = ""
Next i
Word(1).SetFocus
End Sub
```

Word(1).SetFocus moves the cursor (the focus) back to the top word in the list.

After coding your End button, run your program. You will see that to move down the list, you must press Tab or click with the mouse, which is inconvenient if you are typing a list of words.

However, many users are accustomed to pressing Enter after each entry and having the cursor move to the next box automatically. It is easy to add this capability. You have to use the action KeyDown and look for the Enter key. Where would you put the code to do this? (Hint: which control is active when the user is touching Enter?)

Since the user is entering text into a Word text box, the code processing the pressing of the Enter key goes into Word_KeyDown ( ).

```
Sub Word_KeyDown (index As Integer, keycode As ⇒
   Integer, Shift As)
     If keycode = 13 Or keycode = 40 Then 'ENTER or ⇒
     cursor right
        index = index + 1                    'next box
        If index > 20 Then index = 1         'wrap from ⇒
           bottom to top
     End If
     'add code for cursor left here!        'cursor left key
                                            'previous box
                                            'don't go below 1


     Word(index).SetFocus                   'move cursor ⇒
        to selected box
  End Sub
```

Now run the program. Does Enter or the right-arrow key behave like the Tab key? For some reason, Visual Basic beeps when you press Enter in a text box. If you experimented with the small program in Section 9.2, you may have discovered that the KeyPress event happens after the KeyDown event. (In Visual Basic jargon, a keypress is not completed until the key is released. Therefore KeyDown executes before **KeyPress**.)

Fortunately, Visual Basic emits the beep after KeyPress occurs, when KeyUp detects a character 13. Therefore, you can get rid of the sound by persuading the computer that the user never pressed Enter. To do so, set the **KeyAscii** value of an Enter KeyPress:

```
Sub Word_KeyPress (index As Integer, KeyAscii As ⇒
   Integer)
     If KeyAscii = 13 Then KeyAscii = 0
  End Sub
```

You have already processed the Enter key, so changing the key's value now doesn't affect anything but the beep.

Modifications

1. Experiment to see what the code is for the cursor up-arrow key and add a routine to process it. Follow the previously described pattern, but make the index less rather than more. Don't go below zero.

2. Does the sort routine work properly if some of the words have leading spaces? Use LTRIM to cut them off. (See Chapter 8.)

Enhancement

Provide the user with a choice of sort direction. Add two option buttons, Ascending and Descending. Alter the Sort routine accordingly.

Exercises

At your desk

1. The swap routine in Section 9.1 looks like this:

```
If Letter$(L) > Letter$(R) Then          'if left card >
  right card
    temp$ = Letter$(L)              'save left card
    Letter$(L) = Letter$(R)        'put right card into ⇒
      left "hand"
    Letter$(R) = temp$             'pick up saved (left) ⇒
      card in right
End If
```

This routine introduces a variable called `temp$`. Suppose that you want to swap two variables. Why couldn't you use the following?

```
Letter$(L) = Letter$(R)
Letter$(R) = Letter$(L)
```

If `Letter$(L)`'s value is 20 and `Letter$(R)` equals 12 before the preceding switch, what would each variable's value be after the switch?

2. What would be the values of each element of the num array after you run the following routine? (Be careful, this is not a full sort routine; you have to track it.)

```
num(1) = 5 : num(2) = 2 : num(3) = 3 : num(4) = 3
  num(5) = 1
For i = 1 To 4
   If num(i) > num(i + 1) Then
       temp = num(i)
       num(i) = num(j)
       num(j) = temp
   End If
Next i
```

3. You have two buttons: DoMuchButton and DoLittleButton. In the code for DoMuchButton_Click, in addition to its own function, you wish to cause the same thing to happen as if DoLittleButton had been pressed. To accomplish this, instead of duplicating the DoLittleButton's code, what single line do you place in DoMuchButton_Click?

4. In a sentence, explain how you would have a program set up an array of buttons, DoThisButton(1) to DoThisButton(5). What is the first thing that you must do? What Visual Basic statement is required to create a new button?

5. You have dimensioned an array: `Dim A$(10):`

```
UpButton_Click ()
   index = index + 1
   Label1.Caption = A$(index)
End If
```

When the user clicks on UpButton, Label1's caption changes. Modify the accompanying code to ensure that the index does not get too high. Assume that `index` and the `A$( )` array are global variables (and thus are known to the UpButton_Click routine).

6. You have a form that contains some buttons. What statement could you put in Form_Load to give the EndButton the focus, so that merely pressing Enter would trigger the EndButton? (This chapter demonstrated two methods of accomplishing this.)

At your computer

Create a form that accepts the marks for three subjects (prices for three objects, and the times for three runners) as shown in Figure 10-10. When the user clicks the Sort button, the numbers and the labels (subjects, objects, and runners) change as shown in Figure 10-11.

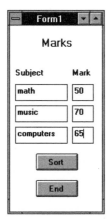

Figure 10-10
Data being entered into the form

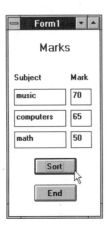

Figure 10-11
The form after sorting the entered data

Make the cursors jump across each line when the user presses Tab. That is, the focus should move from subject 1 to mark 1, subject 2, mark 2, and so on.

Bonus: MakeAllow the pressing of Enter to work similarly to the pressing of Tab.

Caution: Many users will swap the marks but leave the subject names unchanged.

Try your program and make sure that 11 is a higher mark than 9. If not, you need to use **Val** in SortButton_Click. (The value 11 is bigger than 9, but the string 11 is less than 9, because 1 comes before 9.)

Chapter 11 Using the Common Dialog Box and Sequential Files

Many applications write information to a disk or a hard drive for retrieval later. In this chapter, you see how to write a program that accesses information on your disk.

11.1 The common dialog box

Most applications that read and write to disk have a module that enables the user to specify the drive, directory, and name of a file. Visual Basic provides a custom control, the common dialog box, for you to use to perform this task.[1] This control provides your program with several familiar boxes. One is the Open dialog box shown in Figure 11-1.

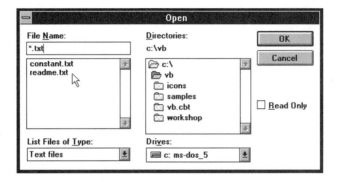

Figure 11-1
The common dialog box for requesting the name of the file

There are other types of common dialog boxes. Depending on the number assigned to the box's Action property, the box that appears can be the standard box for opening a file (type 1, in Figure 1.11), saving a file (2), selecting a color (3), selecting a font (4), printing (5), or displaying Windows Help screens (6).

To see the common dialog box in action, create the simple form shown in Figure 11-2.

---

[1]Visual Basic 1.0 did not contain a common dialog box. You had to combine on a form three separate controls: the file, drive, and directory list box. The manual gave a complete listing for constructing a file open or save dialog box.

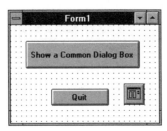

Figure 11-2
Sampling the CMDialog box

Create two buttons. Then select the common dialog box control and place it on the form. The location of the control icon doesn't matter because the control never appears when the program runs. Your coding causes the window containing the dialog box to open.

As you would expect in Visual Basic, the code for operating the common dialog box is attached to the control that causes the dialog box to open. Therefore, you enter the following instructions in **Sub** ShowButton_Click ( ):

```
Sub ShowButton_Click ()
    x = InputBox("Enter the type of Common Dialog Box, ⇒
       from 1 to 6, or 0 for none")

    Select Case x
       Case 1, 2
          CMDialog1.Filename = ""    'clear any ⇒
             previous name
          CMDialog1.Filter = "All files (*.*) | *.*"
          CMDialog1.Action = x       'opens the box

          If CMDialog1.Filename = "" Then
             MsgBox ("No file selected")
          Else
             MsgBox ("You chose " + CMDialog1.Filename)
          End If
       Case 3
          CMDialog1.Flags = &H1&
          CMDialog1.Action = 3        'opens the box
          Form1.BackColor = CMDialog1.Color 'sets ⇒
             the color
       Case 4
          On Error GoTo NotReadyYet
          CMDialog1.Action = 4
       Case 5
          CMDialog1.Action = 5
       Case 6
          GoTo NotReadyYet
       Case Else
    End Select
    Exit Sub
```

```
NotReadyYet:
    MsgBox ("Other parameters must be set for this to ⇒
        work")
    Exit Sub
End Sub
```

Code your Quit button and run the program.

For types 1 and 2 dialog boxes, **MsgBox** shows that the dialog box passed a file name back to the program.

The color selection dialog box works. However, the font message box does not behave properly, because you have omitted several initial settings. In fact, the message box generates a Visual Basic run-time error. The message box itself generates the first message box that appears, mentioning missing fonts. The second message comes from your program. If you comment out (prefix with an apostrophe) to the **On Error GoTo** line, the program crashes after the dialog box's message. **On Error GoTo** intercepts errors that might prevent your program from continuing.

11.2 Trapping program and user errors

As the last paragraph indicates, some errors can crop up in a program at run time that cause the program to terminate with an error message on the screen. In general, you don't want these errors to happen. Your applications should catch problems and deal with them before a serious run-time error occurs.

For example, suppose that you have a calculation that divides the variable distance by the variable time. If time happens to equal zero, the program crashes with a "Division by Zero" error. Your program's users would lose any information that they did not save.

One way to prevent this error, of course, is to be careful to check for zero before dividing:

```
If time <>0 then
    speed = distance / time
Else
    MsgBox "Please enter the time for the trip"
    speed = 0
End If
```

The **On Error GoTo** statement enables you to trap errors that you, the programmer, did not foresee:

```
Sub CalculateSomething ()
On Error GoTo ErrorTrap

... your program continues here

Exit Sub
ErrorTrap:
```

```
            MsgBox ("There is a problem with the data. This ⇒
               routine cannot be completed.")
        End Sub
```

When the program enters this **Sub**, the **On Error GoTo** statement notifies the program to branch to the ErrorTrap line if an otherwise fatal error occurs. Under that line, you add any statements to deal with the error. These statement could range from informing the user of a problem to skipping the problem lines, such as a line that divides by a variable that unexpectedly has taken on the value of zero.[2]

Every error has an error number, which you can find by examining the value of Err. The Visual Basic reference manual includes a list of the error codes. Your program could check for some common errors, such as trying to write on an write-protected disk or a full disk. For example, a routine that writes data to the disk might use the following:

```
On Error GoTo DiskProblem

    ... program begins to write to disk

Exit Sub

DiskProblem:
    x = Err
    Select Case x
        Case 61
            MsgBox ("Disk is full. Data has not been ⇒
               saved")
            Exit Sub
        Case 70, 71
            choice = MsgBox ("Disk Problem ... Please ⇒
               fix and press Retry, or Cancel", 21)
            If choice = 2 Then     'Cancel was pressed
               MsgBox ("Data not saved")
               Exit Sub
            Else                    'Try again
               Resume
            End If
        Case Else
            MsgBox ("A problem has occurred. Call  555-4567 ⇒
               and report this error number: "+ Str$(x))
    End Select
End Sub
```

---

[2]A good programmer would anticipate this possibility. Instead of a line that simply says

```
    average = total / number
```
the program could have read
```
    If number <> 0 then
       average = total / number
    Else
       deal with the problem
    End if
```

The preceding routine demonstrates the use of the **Resume** statement, which causes the program to continue at the statement where the error occurred. You can also use **Resume Next** to skip the statement that caused the error.

11.3 Storing information in sequential files

Your program can store data for later retrieval in one of two types of disk files: sequential and random access. You use a sequential file to store an array of numbers or letters, a selection of text of variable length, or a single character, number, or word on the disk. In most cases, your program reads a sequential file from the beginning, searching for needed data. In other cases, your program reads an entire sequential file from the disk and into the computer's memory. You usually don't use a sequential file to store names, addresses, and phone numbers of all 20,000 of your friends, because that would be too much data for the computer to hold in memory at one time, and searching through a file one friend at a time is inefficient. A random access file, which is explained in Chapter 12, is a better choice for this job.

You could use a sequential file to store the date that a program was last used, the names and scores of the top 10 players of your computer game, this week's message that is to appear on the bottom of invoices generated by the computer, or the current password (encrypted) for your payroll program. Let's look at one of these examples.

Suppose that you write for a client a program that, when run, displays the date of last use. How can a program know when it was last run? Sequential files provide a method. All the program needs to do is to write the date on the disk or hard drive just before exiting. On startup, the program reads the file and inputs the date:

```
'user has selected Quit
Open "SAVEDATE.TXT" For Output As #1
    Print #1, DATE$
Close #1
```

In this code, the **Open** line creates a file called **SAVEDATE.TXT** on the disk. You, as the programmer, assign a file number, **#1**. This number is arbitrary; you could use **#5** instead, as long as you use the same number in subsequent statements. The **Print** statement places **Date$**, a Visual Basic function, in file **#1**, and the **Close** statement completes the operation. (Advanced note: The **Print #** statement writes the information to a file buffer. The program writes the information to disk only when the buffer is full. The **Close** statement writes any unwritten data to disk. If you fail to close the file, you might lose some information.)

When the program runs, it must read the data:

```
'user has selected Quit
Open "SAVEDATE.TXT" For Input As #2
    Input #2, A$
Close #2
Print "Date of last use of this program: ";A$
```

This example uses **#2** as the file number just to demonstrate that the file number itself need not be the same as the original. Note the **For Input** instead of **For Output**, the **Input #** instead of **Print #**, and **A$** instead of **Date$**. The variable name can differ from the original too. (You cannot use **Date$**, because that would cause the system clock's date to change.)

The example has one logical flaw: the routine that writes the date to disk comes at the end of the program, and the routine that reads the date from disk comes at the beginning. (After all, if you write the date out first, only to read it in again, the date of last use would always be the current date.) So how do you get the original date on the disk before the first use of the program?

You have several options. One is to place a phrase on the disk before giving the program to your client. You could use a text editor (like **DOS EDIT**) to write something such as "Never used before" on the disk in the file **SAVEDATE.TXT**. Or, you could just use a program consisting of the three-line output routine shown earlier in this section. A more sophisticated method is to check for the presence of **SAVEDATE.TXT** on the directory and, if no such file exists, abort the file input routine. Here is the code:

```
Sub ReadTheFile ()

    On Error GoTo NoFileThere

    Open "SAVEDATE.TXT" For Input As #2
        Input #2, A$
    Close #2
Afterread:
    On Error GoTo 0
    MsgBox "Date of last use of this program: "+A$

    'program continues

Exit Sub

NoFileThere:
    A$= "This is the first use of the program"
Resume Afterread
End Sub
```

When the program first runs, it generates an error when it tries to read in the nonexistent date data. The **On Error** line tells the program to branch to the error recovery routine at the line **NoFileThere**. The **Resume** command tells the program where to continue. The **On Error GoTo 0** line turns off this error-trapping routine. In complex programs, you would leave error trapping on, pointing to some other error-recovery routine:

```
On Error GoTo GeneralErrorTrap
```

Sequential files are often used to hold arrays. Suppose that you have an array of names stored in N$( ) and have used the integer variable n to hold the number of names. That is, N$(1) is the first name, N$(2) the second, up to N$(n), which is the last name.

Here is the file-write routine:

```
Open "NAMES.FLE" For Output As #1
    Print #1, n
    For i = 1 To n
        Print #1, N$(i)³
    Next i
Close #1
```

Here is the file-read routine:

```
Open "NAMES.FLE" For Input As #1
    Input #1, n
    For i = 1 To n
        Input #1, N$(i)
    Next i
Close #1
```

If you don't know how many names are in the file, you can use a special function called **EOF(1)**, standing for *end of file #1*. Suppose that, unlike the above example, NAMES.FLE contains just the names, but no integer that represents the number of names. Here's how to read them:

```
Open "NAMES.FLE" For Input As #1
    i = 0
    Do While Not EOF(1)
        i = i + 1                        'increase i
        Input #1, N$(i)
    Loop
Close #1
```

If your names contain commas, quotation marks, or colons, you must take special care. If N$(1) were written as *Smythe, Rob*, then the preceding routine would read back *Smythe* as N$(1) and *Rob* as N$(2), because commas are valid separators between items in a list that an **Input** statement will retrieve.

There are two ways around this problem. One is to use quotation marks in the file write routine. A quotation mark (**"**) is a **Chr$(34)**. The following is a safer output routine than the original:

```
Open "NAMES.FLE" For Output As #1
    Print #1, n
    For i = 1 To n
        Print #1, CHR$(34);N$(i);CHR$(34)
    Next i
Close #1
```

---

[3] The computer adds a carriage return, or Enter, at the end of any **Print#** statement that does not end in a semicolon or comma.

You need not change the input routine. The quotation marks will not be included in the input strings. This routine will not work, however, if the strings themselves contain quotation marks. If this is a possibility, use **Line Input**, which takes in all text up to a carriage routine (a **Chr$(13)**, or Enter). A **Chr$(13)** is automatically placed after each line, unless the line ends in a semicolon. Therefore, a **Chr$(13)** is the file after each N$(i).

```
Open "NAMES.FLE" For Input As #1
    Input #1, n
    For i = 1 To n
        Line Input #1, N$(i)
    Next i
Close #1
```

You could also use **Write #** instead of **Print #**. **Write #** places quotation marks around each output string itself and inserts comma delimiters between fields.

Finally, another way to bring in saved characters from a text file is to get them one at a time. Application 11 demonstrates this technique.

Application 11 Making, saving, and retrieving a text file

Overview

The user can enter text, save it on disk, and retrieve it later. The user can also open and edit a text file. While editing, the user can search for a specific string of characters in the file.

Learning objectives

- using common dialog open and save boxes
- writing and reading sequential files
- creating pulldown menus
- using MsgBox and InputBox
- enabling and disabling menu items
- selecting text
- using Instr( ) to see whether a string contains a target character
- using Mid$ and Len string functions
- using On Error, Resume, and Error$
- using Input$ to read a single character from a file

Instructions

Figure 11-3 shows the application's form. It has two labels: Label1 contains the title at the top, and Label2 displays brief user instructions at the bottom. The form also has a large text box called Contents. Set the box's Multiline property to **True** and the scroll bars to 2 (vertical).

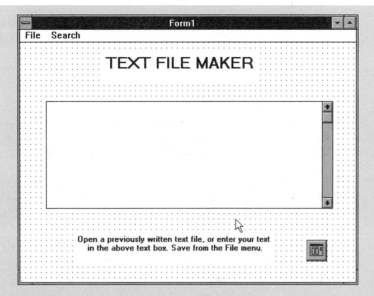

Figure 11-3
The form for Application 11

The form also contains a pulldown menu. Figure 11-4 shows its structure. The & signs in the menu choice names indicate Alt+letter keys. These are underlined when the user pulls down the menu. The user can make a selection by pressing Alt plus the underlined letter. To insert a separation line in the menu, include a line that contains only a hyphen. The Names for each menu choice are FileChoice, NewChoice, OpenChoice, SaveChoice, SaveAsChoice, sep1 (the hyphen line), and ExitChoice.

Figure 11-4
The menu structure

Place a common dialog box on the form. Set its CancelError property to **True**.

Add the following routine for the File menu's New command:

```
Sub NewChoice_Click ()
   Contents.Text = ""
   SaveAsChoice.Enabled = 0
   SaveChoice.Enabled = 0
End Sub
```

The last two statements disable saving if there is no file to save. The menu items will be printed in light colors and be inoperable. To turn on the saving menu items, you can look for the presence of text in Text1.Text every time that a change is made:

```
Sub Text1_Change ()
   If Len(Contents.Text) > 0 Then
      SaveAsChoice.Enabled = 1: SaveChoice.Enabled = 1
   Else
      SaveAsChoice.Enabled = 0: SaveChoice.Enabled = 0
   End IF
End Sub
```

Add the following routine for the File menu's Open command:

```
Sub OpenChoice_Click ()
   CMDialog1.Filter = "Text files (*.txt)|*.txt|Batch ⇒
      files (*.bat)|*.bat"              'the type of ⇒
         files to be displayed
   CMDialog1.FilterIndex = 1
   CMDialog1.Action = 1
   file$ = CMDialog1.Filename
   If file$ <> "" Then
      filltextbox
      SaveAsChoice.Enabled = True
      SaveChoice.Enabled = True
   End If
End Sub
```

The preceding routine refers to a named **Sub** called filltextbox, which reads in the chosen file and displays it in the window. Place it in general declarations:

```
Sub filltextbox ()

   inputstring$ = ""
   Contents.Text = "Loading the file ... a moment ⇒
      please"
   On Error GoTo NoSuchFile
   Open file$ For Input As #1 ' Open file.
```

```
      Do While Not EOF(1)
          char$ = Input$(1, #1)        ' Get one character.
          Select Case char$
             Case Chr$(13) ' If enter (carriage return)
                'do nothing (i.e. filter it out)
             Case Chr$(10) ' If line feed,
                 inputstring$ = inputstring$ + Chr$(13) + Chr$(10)
             Case Else          ' If not line feed or enter add to line.
                 inputstring$ = inputstring$ + char$
          End Select
      Loop  ' Loop if not at end-of-file.
   Close #1 ' Close file.
   Contents.Text = inputstring$
   Exit Sub

NoSuchFile:
   MsgBox ("No such file as " + file$)

   Resume Bottom
Bottom:
End Sub
```

The preceding routine opens the file and, until the end-of-file character is called, reads in one character at a time. The routine examines the character to see whether it's a line feed (Chr$(10)) or carriage return (Chr$(13)). If not, the character is added to inputstring$. The routine filters out carriage returns, but adds a combination of line feed plus charriage return characters to the input-string$. When a string is printed, the linefeed causes the cursor to drop down a line and the return moves it to the start of the line.

Under the File menu's Save command you put the code needed for writing to a file. If no file name has been previously used, you use the SaveAsChoice_Click routine to bring up the common dialog box and ask for a file name:

```
Sub SaveAsChoice_Click ()
    CMDialog1.Action = 2
    If file$ <> "" Then WriteFile
End Sub

Sub SaveChoice_Click ()
   If file$ = "" Then
      Call SaveAsChoice_Click
   Else
      WriteFile
   End If
End Sub
```

The two save routines include WriteFile, another general subroutine:

```
Sub WriteFile ()
    Open File$ For Output As #1 ' Open file.
        For i = 1 To Len(Contents.Text)
            Print #1, Mid$Contents.Text, i, 1);'⁴
    Next i
    Print #1, ""
    Close #1 ' Close file.
End Sub
```

The write and read routines need to use the value of `File$` obtained from the common dialog box. Make `File$` a global variable by adding one line to general declarations:

```
Dim File$
```

The Search menu choice provides an example of the use of SelStart and SelLength:

```
Sub SearchChoice_Click ()
    msg$ = "Find what string of characters?"
    Title$ = "Search"
    searchstring$ = InputBox$(msg$, Title$) ' Get user input.
    x = InStr(Contents.text, searchstring$) 'position of string
    If x > 0 Then                       'if the searchstring is present
        Contents.SelStart = x - 1         'start highlighting here
        Contents.SelLength = Len(searchstring$)  'highlight ⇒
            this many characters
    Else
        Beep
        msg$ = "Not found"
        MsgBox msg$, 0, "Results of search"
    End If
End Sub
```

In the preceding code, the function `Instr(largestring$, target$)` *evaluates to a number. If the number is zero, the* `target$` *is not contained in the* `largestring$`. *If the* `target$` *is present, the number is the position of the first letter of* `target$`. *For example,* `Instr("Good morning", "or")` *equals 7. SelStart and SelLength go together. Characters are automatically highlighted beginning at SelStart. SelLength specifies the number of characters to highlight.*

Finally, add code to ExitChoice_Click. An **"Are You Sure?"** question is suitable here.

---

⁴ The semicolon at the end of the Print # statement above prevents a carriage return (a `Chr$(13)`) from being added after the character that has been written to the file. The effect is to join all characters sent into one long string, exactly the same characters as were contained in Contents.Text.

Modifications	Save Contents.Text as soon as it is placed in the text box. When the user attempts to exit, compare the current contents with the saved contents to see whether a change has been made. If so, warn the user and ask whether he or she wants to save the new text.

Exercises

At your desk

1. The common dialog box is a tool that performs some familiar tasks that you have seen in various programs. What are the six tasks for which you can use the common dialog box control?

2. If an error condition occurs in a running program, the program crashes unless you trap the error. You can add a statement to intercept the error and direct your program to some code that you have written to handle errors. What statement would you use to cause the program to jump to the line statement ErrorHandler in the event of an error?

3. What statement must you use to exit an error-handling routine and continue the program where you left off?

4. What statements would you use to create on your disk a sequential file that contains your name?

5. The following routine writes to a disk file 10 random integer numbers between 1 and 10:

```
Open "Numbers.txt" For Output as #1
     For i = 1 to 10
        Print #1, Int(Rnd * 10 + 1)
     Next i
Close #1
```

What statements would you use to read the numbers into your file?

6. What would be the output of this two-line program?

```
a$ = "Therefore"
Print Instr(a$, "or")
```

At your computer

1. Create an application that asks for a file name and displays on-screen the name of the file that you select. The form shown in Figure 11-5 is suitable. When you press the appropriate button, a common dialog box appears asking you which file to open. The file appears in the label below the word Result. (You need not actually write the code to open the file.)

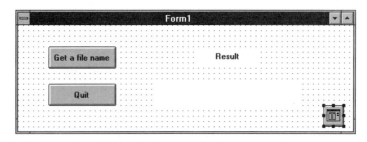

Figure 11-5
A form that displays a file name

2. Most computers have a file called C:\CONFIG.SYS that contains instructions that the computer uses when it boots. Write a program to display the contents of your CONFIG.SYS file on the screen. Figure 11-6 shows the form, which contains a picture box and two buttons. (Make sure that you open the CONFIG.SYS file for input only.)

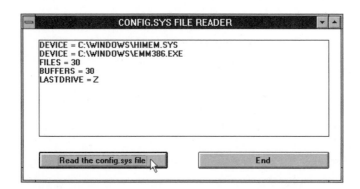

Figure 11-6
The contents of the CONFIG.SYS file inside a picture box

A simple way to display a line of text in a picture box is to use the following **Print** statement:

```
Picture1.Print a$
```

Chapter 12 Using Random Access Files

In Chapter 11 you learned about sequential files. Letters written with your word processor are examples of sequential files: the information is written to the disk in one long set of characters. In general, you open such files, read the information from the beginning, and close the file.

In this chapter you learn to use random access files. After opening such files, your program can read information from the middle of the file without having to input all the data in the file to that point. You can, for example, read from the disk file the name and address of your two hundredth customer without having to input the first one hundred and ninty nine.

In order to do this, you use a special type of variable for your customer's data.

12.1 Designer variables: Using the Type statement

You have seen integer, string, and floating-point (decimal) variables. Floating-point variables are usually single precision, unless you want to work with more digits. For greater accuracy, there are two types of variables that store more digits: double-precision floating-point variables and long integers.

You can design a variable that combines all these variable types. For example, instead of saving people's names, addresses, and ages in arrays called Name$, Address$, City, and Age, you can define one type of variable called Person that holds these four variables:

```
Type Person
    Name As String * 20   'note: no $ needed because ⇒
        defined as String
    Address As String * 20
    City As String * 10
    Age As Integer
End Type
```

Person is a *type* of variable, not a variable name, just as integer is a type of variable rather than a variable name. If you define a variable name such as Client to be a variable of the type Person, Client would have four *fields*: Client.Name, Client.Address, Client.City, and Client.Age. Notice that a period separates the fields from the variable name (just as a period separates a control's properties from the control's name). Client's four fields consist of three strings, adding to a total of 50 characters, and an integer, which requires two characters.

The Type statement is a *module*-level instruction. It is not attached to the form. You must open File and choose New Module. This command adds a file called Module1.bas to the project window. When you save your project and form, you rename and save the module file. By defining a variable type Person in a module, you make that structure of variable available to all subprocedures in all forms that make up your project.

You declare your variable Client to be of type Person in the general declarations section of your program:

```
Dim Client as Person
```

You could also declare an array to be of type Person:

```
Dim Customer(100) as Person
```

This **Dim** statement defines an array Customer for 100 customers, each with a name, address, city, and age.

A string field must be large enough to hold the maximum number of letters that you expect or want to allow for that field. You must handle numeric fields a bit differently. Integers up to ± 32767 take two characters (even one-digit numbers), and single-precision floating-point (decimal) numbers take four. Double-precision integers take four, and double-precision floating-point variables take eight.

Type variables not only are useful for associating several different quantities (for example, a name and an address), they are essential for the use of random access files.

12.2 Random access files

You have seen that a sequential disk file consists of a series of numbers or strings written consecutively. Although there are ways of positioning to begin reading from the middle of a sequential file, the usual procedure is to open the file and read the data items one after another. To retrieve item 20, for example, you read and ignore 19 items, then read and use the next one. Sequential files are good for storing items quickly in a minimum of disk space. Examples are storing the names and high scores for an arcade game, or saving some changeable data, such as your system's type of monitor and modem or your current password, that your program needs to read when first run.

Advanced computer note: Sequential files can hold very large amounts of data. If the program is going to process the items in sequence, storing them in a sequential file and reading them one at a time is no problem. Also, if the program knows the pattern (for example, that each item is six characters long), you can have the computer read an item from the middle of the file by calculating its position in the file and reading from that point. In general, however, you use sequential files for saving documents, arrays of values, lists, and series of statements.

For very large amounts of data organized in some pattern, random access files are better. Suppose that you have to store and retrieve the data for thousands of clients' names, addresses, and phone numbers. That would be too much data to hold in the computer's memory at the same time. You would not want to have to read through all the data for 500 clients to retrieve the 501st. A random access file enables you to tell the computer to bring in only the name, address, and phone number of client 501. You could work with that data, save it, and bring in the data for client 10 just as easily as for client 502. You need not retrieve data from random access files sequentially; you can read the file in random order.

Although a sequential file's structure is totally flexible, a random access file has an overall organization: it consists of similar *records*. Each record contains the entire contents of a single variable that you have defined in a **Type** statement. In the previous example, each client's data would go into a separate record. The record would consist of fields: one for the name, one for the address, one for the city, and one for the age. Each record is identical in length and structure, even if the names have different lengths. When you define the structure of variable type Person, you specify in advance how much space the computer is to allocate for the four fields. That's how the computer can retrieve the data for client 501: it knows how long a record is and can jump to the right place in the random access file to bring in the next four items, which will be the requested name, address, city, and age.

A random access file can waste space. Long names occupy the same space as short names. However, random access files enable your computer to retrieve specific records more easily and quickly.

Continue with the sample variable declarations presented in Section 12.1:

```
Type Person
   Name As String * 20
   Address As String * 20
   City As String * 10
   Age As Integer
End Type

Dim Client as Person
Dim Customer(100) as Person
```

Suppose that you obtained the following data for your client:

```
Client.Name = "Dori Shen"
Client.Address = "123 Main Street"
Client.City = "Paris"
Client.Age = 25
```

Here is the routine for writing the entire Client data into its own record in a random access file. The file name is CLIENTS.DAT and `rec` is an integer that holds the record number into which the computer is to place the data.

```
Open "CLIENTS.DAT" For Random As #1 Len = 52
Put #1, rec, Client 'write the fields of client to ⇒
  disk in record rec
Close #1
```

Any variable of type Person requires 52 bytes (memory locations) to store all four fields. You determine this number by adding the sizes of the fields in the **Type** statement. Therefore, to store all the client data requires a record size of 52. The **Open** statement for the random access file declares the following:

```
Open "CLIENTS.DAT" For Random As #1 Len = 52
```

This **Open** statement is similar to that for sequential files, except that it uses the word **Random** rather than **Input** or **Output** and specifies the record's length.

Now you must write the record to disk. If rec equals 3, for example, the following command would write the client data into record 3:[1]

```
Put #1, rec, Client
```

Finally, you close the file:

```
Close #1, rec
```

Important: The program may not actually write the data to disk until it reaches the **Close** statement. If the program ends after the **Put** statement but fails to close the file, you probably will lose the data. See footnote 1.

Here is the corresponding code for retrieving the data from the record `rec`:

```
Open "CLIENTS.DAT" For Random As #1 Len = 52
   Get #1, rec, Client
Close #1
```

You could bring the contents of the record rec into a different variable, as long as it is of the same **Type** as `Client`. For example, if a `Customer` array was of **Type** Person (the type that you defined for `Client`), you could retrieve `Customer(i)`'s data from the record rec as follows:

```
Open "CLIENTS.DAT" For Random As #1 Len = 52
   Get #1, rec, Customer(i)
Close #1
```

---

[1] Actually, the data might not get written to disk until the file is closed. The data is first put into a *buffer*, a set of memory locations that hold the data until sufficient characters have accumulated to cause the computer to access the disk. When the buffer is full, or when the program reaches the **Close** statement, the data is copied from the buffer to the disk. If you omit the **Close** statement, you can lose data.

Application 12 **Using random access files**

Application 12 uses a random access file and a sequential file and lays the foundation for Programming Adventure 2.

Overview

The user can enter names and addresses of friends, save the data to disk, and then retrieve the names and addresses later.

Learning Objectives

- writing and reading sequential files
- using random access files
- using InputBox$
- enabling and disabling buttons
- using frames
- using Type to define variables
- using On Error GoTo for error checking

Instructions

The form has two frames, 10 labels, and five buttons (see Figure 12-1). Make the two frames first, then place the labels, text boxes, and the Add button on the large frame, and three labels on the bottom frame.

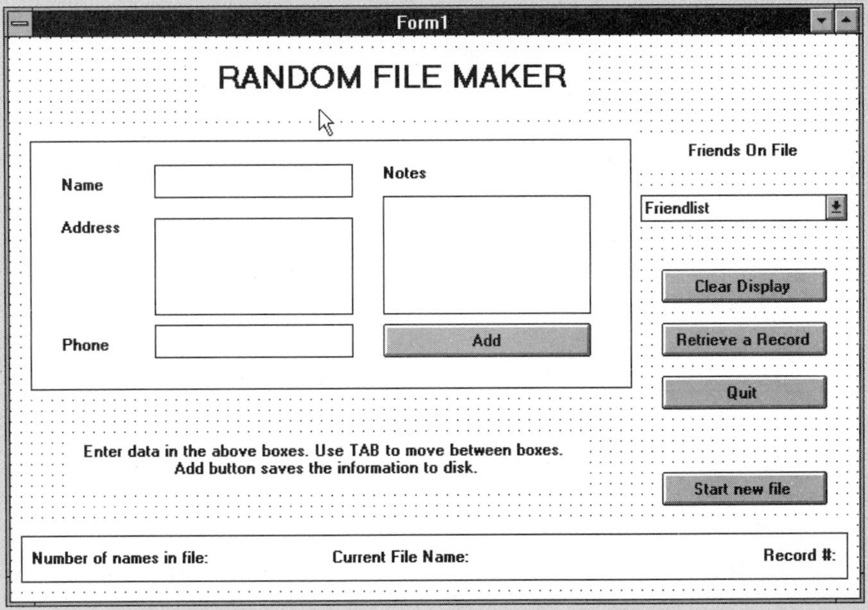

Figure 12-1
The random file maker form

If you make the controls before making the frame, you find that the frame goes on top of the controls, not behind them. Also, the controls would not be fixed on the frame. To recover without redoing everything, first draw a frame to the side. Then, one by one, cut each control, click on the frame, and paste the object. It will now be connected to the frame. After you have transferred all controls, you can expand and move the frame, dragging all items to their proper positions.

Call the text boxes (not the labels) on the large frame NameBox, AddressBox, PhoneBox, and NotesBox. You should set the large text boxes' MultiLine property to **True**. This setting enables the user to press Enter to place text on more than one line.

Name the boxes on the lower frame NumBox, FileBox, and RecordBox. Set Record.Box's alignment for right-justification.

The combo box on the right, FriendList, is a Style 2 box. This means that the user can select an item from the pulldown list but cannot type an entry on the top line.

Call the buttons AddButton, Clearbutton, RetrieveButton, QuitButton, and NewButton.

Now add the code. To help you understand how everything works, explanations accompany each procedure.

Start by viewing the code for your file. Add the following:

```
Type FriendRecord          ' Create user-defined type.
    FriendName As String * 35
    Address As String * 100
    Phone As String * 15
    Note As String * 150
End Type
```

This creates a special type of variable, which in this case consists of four strings. Just as you could declare a variable FirstName *to be a string, after you define FriendRecord you can declare a variable such as* OnePerson *to be a variable of type FriendRecord. This would give* OnePerson *four string components that any variable of type FriendRecord is to have:* OnePerson.Friendname, *a 35-character string;* OnePerson.Address, *a 100-character string;* OnePerson.Phone, *a 15-character string; and* OnePerson.Note, *a 150-character string.*

Declare OnePerson, and other variables, in general declarations:

```
Dim Shared OnePerson As FriendRecord

Dim Shared Friend(30) As String
Dim Shared InRecord(30) As Integer
Dim Shared FriendName As String
Dim Shared Address As String
Dim Shared Phone As String
Dim Shared Note As String
Dim Shared NumInList As Integer
Dim Shared record
```

These declarations also ensure that all subprocedures share the variables friendname, address, phone, note, NumInList, *and* record. *You also declare two arrays:* Friend( ) *can hold as many as 30 names, and* InRecord( ) *can hold up to 30 integers.* InRecord(i) *holds the record number of the* ith *name in the random access file that you will create. (The arrays can actually hold 31 items, because you can have subscript zero.)*

This program uses two files. FRIENDS.SEQ is a sequential array that holds the number of names on file, the names, and the record numbers that indicate in which record the rest of the persons' data are stored in the random access file FRIENDS.RND.

Here is how the program generally works after some prior use:

- The form loads, reading the sequential file. The program learns how many items it previously saved (NumInList), reads the names into the Friend( ) array, and reads into the InRecord( ) array the pointers that indicate the record in which each name is located. The program also displays the names in the drop-down combo box.

- After adding a new person's data, the program increases the number of items, adds the name to the Friend( ) array, sets InRecord(NumInList) to an unused record number, and stores the new data in that record number. Finally, the program adds the person's name to the combo box.

- If the user selects a name from the combo box, the program reads the random access file and displays the data for possible modification.

- An added feature allows recovery of the data from the random file without using the combo box. When the user begins typing in the name box, if the keystrokes happen to match a stored name, the program brings that person's data into memory and displays it.

Although the InRecord( ) *array is redundant in Application 12, you use the array in Programming Adventure 2, which expands on Application 12.*

Enter the code for Form_Load to read the sequential file when the program first runs:

```
Sub Form_Load ()
    On Error GoTo startnewfile
        filebox.Caption = "File: FRIENDS.RND"
        Open "Friends.seq" For Input As #1
            Input #1, NumInList

            For i = 1 To NumInList
                Input #1, Friend(i)
                Input #1, InRecord(i)
                FriendList.AddItem RTrim$(Friend(i))
            Next i
```

```
            Close #1
            NumBox.Caption = "Number of names in file:" + ⇒
               Str$(NumInList)
         Exit Sub

   startnewfile:
      Close #1
      Open "friends.seq" For Output As #1
         Print #1, 0
      Close #1
      On Error GoTo 0
      Resume

   End Sub
```

This routine illustrates a technique for the first use of a program that must read a file. Trying to input a number from a nonexistent file generates an error. The **On Error** *line causes execution to jump to the error routine at* startnewfile. *The code here creates a file with a leading zero, to represent the zero items in the file.* **Resume** *causes the program to try again to open and read the sequential file. This time, and all subsequent times, the read succeeds and the program continues. The* On Error GoTo 0 *statement disables error trapping so that this procedure breaks with an error message the next time the program detects an error. This prevents an infinite loop (error, resume, error, resume, and so on) or a jump to the error-trapping routine for an error caused by something else.*

NewButton creates a new sequential file:

```
   Sub NewButton_Click ()
      Open "Friends.seq" For Output As #1
         Print #1, 0
      Close #1
      NumInList = 0
      NumBox.Caption = "Number of names in file:" + ⇒
         Str$(NumInList)
      RecordBox.Caption = "Record #:"
   End Sub
```

When NameBox changes, you must check whether the contents are for a new person or match an already existing person. If the person exists, you retrieve that person's data from the file:

```
   Sub NameBox_Change ()
      match = 0
      If NameBox.Text <> "" Then     'if the box is not ⇒
         blank (quote-quote)
            For i = 1 To NumInList          'go through the ⇒
               names in the list
                  If NameBox.Text = Left$(Friend(i),
                     Len(NameBox.Text)) Then
```

```
                    match = I        'set match = which name it is
                Exit For             'jump out of For-Next loop
            End If
        Next i

        If match = 0 Then            'it's a new name
            AddButton.Caption = "Add"
            AddButton.enabled = True
            AddressBox.Text = ""         'quote-quote
            PhoneBox.Text = ""
            NotesBox.Text = ""
            RecordBox.Caption = "Record #: not in file"
        Else                         'the name is already in the list
            GetARecord match         'load in already stored data
            AddButton.Caption = "Update"
            AddButton.enabled = True     'enable AddButton
        End If
    Else                             'name box is blank; blank
      the others
        AddButton.Caption = "" 'erase caption on AddButton
        AddButton.enabled = 0    'disable it
        AddressBox.Text = ""
        PhoneBox.Text = ""
        NotesBox.Text = ""
        RecordBox.Caption = "Record #:"
    End If
End Sub
```

This code refers to a subprogram called GetARecord. You can code that subprogram later. Here's the AddButton code:

```
Sub AddButton_Click ()
    Select Case AddButton.Caption
        Case "Add"                       'go past bottom of list
        record = NumInList + 1
        Case "Update"                    'leave record at its present value
        Case Else
            record = 0
    End Select

    If record <> 0 And NameBox.Text <> "" Then
        If record > NumInList Then    'add to bottom of list
            FriendList.AddItem NameBox.Text
            NumInList = NumInList + 1 'increase number of items
            NumBox.Caption = "Number of names in file:" + Str$(NumInList)
```

```
                                    End If
                                    Friend(record) = NameBox.Text
                                    InRecord(record) = record
                                    OnePerson.friendname = NameBox.Text
                                    OnePerson.address = AddressBox.Text
                                    OnePerson.phone = PhoneBox.Text
                                    OnePerson.note = NotesBox.Text

                             'write record to random file
                                Open "friends.rnd" For Random As #1 Len = 300
                                    Put #1, record, OnePerson
                                Close #1
                                RecordBox.Caption = "Record #:" + Str$(record)

                             'write list in a sequential file
                                Open "friends.seq" For Output As #1
                                    Write #1, NumInList
                                    For i = 1 To NumInList
                                        Write #1, Friend(i)
                                        Write #1, InRecord(i)
                                    Next i
                                Close #1
                            End If
                        End Sub
```

This coding uses the variable OnePerson, which you previously defined. Note
how simple it is to write this variable into the random access file with the **Put**
statement.

Selecting a name from the combo box should cause the program to read and display the appropriate record. Double-click on the combo box and add the following code:

```
Sub FriendList_Change ()
    record = FriendList.listindex
    GetARecord record
End Sub
```

Pressing the RetrieveButton brings up a message asking which record you want to
read and then retrieves it:

```
Sub Retrievebutton_Click ()
    a$ = InputBox$("Which Record do you wish to read?",⇒
    "Search", "0")
```

```
        r = Val(a$)
        If r <> record And r > 0 Then
            record = r
            GetARecord record
        End If
    End Sub
```

Including the the RetrieveButton during program development and testing is useful, just to see exactly what and where the data is. In a finished product, this button would be unnecessary. The user doesn't have to know which record stores the data, but only how to retrieve it from the combo box.

Go to the general declarations to write the GetARecord procedure:

```
Sub GetARecord (r)
    Open "friends.rnd" For Random As #1 Len = 300
        Get #1, r, OnePerson
    Close #1
    NameBox.Text = RTrim$(OnePerson.friendname)
    AddressBox.Text = OnePerson.address
    PhoneBox.Text = OnePerson.phone
    NotesBox.Text = OnePerson.note
    RecordBox.Caption = "Record #:" + Str$(r)
End Sub
```

Finally, add the code for your Quit button:

Modifications

1. You have often displayed an "Are you sure?" message when the user is about to leave an application. Here is another place for a warning message. Pressing the Start a New File button clears the sequential file's entire contents so that all data is lost. Provide a serious cautionary message and a chance to abort the process if the user presses this dangerous button.

2. When you run the program, you see that you can still retrieve old records after you press NewButton. That's because the information in the random file is still on the disk. Add to NewButton_Click an If statement that checks whether `numinlist` is zero. If so, you should provide a message that there is no record to read. You should read the file only if `numinlist` is greater than zero.

3. RetrieveButton's routine should check that the number of the record that the user wants to read is between 1 and `numinlist`.

4. You hardwired the file names FRIENDS.SEQ and FRIENDS.RND into the program (that is, the code explicitly mentions the file names). In the last chapter, you learned how to use the common dialog box control to enable the user to name a file when saving or select a file from the disk. Add this feature.

Enhancements

1. A modification that you hope you never have to use (but for which your clients will be ever grateful if they do need it) is a Recover button. This button's procedure reads the random access file record by record and reconstructs the `Friend()` and `InRecord()` arrays. On reaching the end of the file, the procedure writes a new sequential file to the disk. You may have noticed that the application stores the names in two places: in the sequential file and as the first field (`OnePerson.friendname`) in each record in the random access file. Although this redundancy wastes disk space, it enables you to recover data if the sequential file is erased or becomes corrupted. This practice is highly recommended.

2. If you choose to add a Recover button, you might consider making it do more than automatically reconstruct the sequential file. You could instead display each person's data as you find it and ask the user whether he or she want to recover that particular data. Until you modify the program (in Programming Adventure 2) to make use of the `InRecord()` array, you should write each recovered record to a different random access file (such as FRIENDS.TMP) and, when done, erase the old file (or, to be safer, rename it FRIENDS.OLD) and rename the new one FRIENDS.RND.

Exercises

At your desk

1. When you store numbers in random access files, the number of bytes required to store the number does not depend on the value of the number. In the last column of the following table, fill in the number of bytes required to store each of the variables. (If you had defined the type of each variable in the application, you would not use the variable name's suffix. For example, if you had placed the statement **Dim age As Integer** in the general declarations, you would not need the percent sign.)

Variable Name	Type of Variable	Bytes Required
age% = 12	Integer	
average! = 66.67	Single-precision floating-point (for short decimal numbers)	
pop& = 1234567890123	Long integer	
mass# = 9876.5432101	Double-precision floating point	

2. Write statements that define a new type of variable to hold an item's six-digit serial number and the item's price (a number less than $1,000).

3. What command do you use to begin accessing a random access file called ST,ORE.DAT with records of the length 150?

4. **a.** What command do you use to move the contents of the variable Item into record 5 of the STORE.DAT file?

   b. What command retrieves the contents of the record recnum into the variable Item?

5. **a.** You realize that an error will occur the first time that someone tries to use a new file (because nothing will be in it), so you write an error-trapping routine beginning at the line FirstUse. What statement do you use to tell the computer to jump to the line FirstUse if an error occurs?

   b. You decide to deal with the error mentioned in question 5(a) by placing a zero in the file, then telling the computer to return to the line that caused the error. Here is the routine:

```
FirstUse:
    Close #1 'because it was Open when error
      occurred
    Open file$ For Output As #1
       Print #1, 0
    Close #1
    On Error GoTo 0
    Open file$ For Input As #1
```

   What command do you use at the end of the preceding routine to have the program return to the line that caused the problem and try to read the file again?

   c. If the program jumps to the error-trapping routine for a different reason than you anticipated, your program's attempt to fix the problem might not work. This could produce an infinite loop, with the program forever jumping between the line that caused the problem and the error-trapping routine. What statement does the preceding routine include to prevent such a loop by stopping the program and stating the error on the screen?

At your computer

Make a program that demonstrates that you know how to save the user's data into a random access file and recover it. The following figures show sample screens for one such program. Figure 12-2 shows data that has been saved to record 4, and Figure 12-3 shows data retrieved from record 2.

Figure 12-2
The program showing that data has been stored in record 4

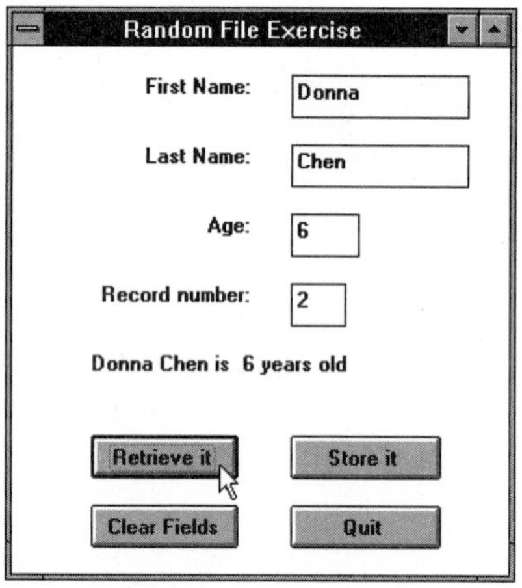

Figure 12-3
The program showing that record 2 has been retrieved

A Visual Basic function that you might want to use is **RTrim$(**FirstNameBox.Text**)**, which removes the spaces from the right side of a caption or text box. This function produces the message with no extra spaces between first and last names.

Figure 12-4 shows that, before attempting to save anything, the program checks to make sure that the user entered a record number.

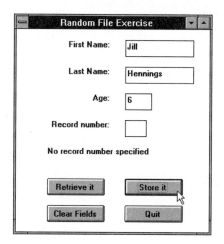

Figure 12-4
The form displays a message if the user did not enter a record number

Other possible features of this program include checking whether the name and age boxes have data in them before writing the data to disk, and announcing when the user has attempted to read from an empty record.

Programming Adventure 2
Expense Tracker

The three-form application that you create in this programming adventure is quite interesting and informative. You use both a sequential and a random access file, Visual Basic's built-in date and printer routines, and different fonts. You create a "hidden password" entry form, which you can use in any other applications, and you learn a little about encryption.

PA2.1 Using a sequential file to index a random access file

Suppose that you have stored the names, addresses, phone numbers, and birthdays for your 20,000 friends in a large random access file called FRIENDS.RND. You want to find out when Ray Buie's birthday is. How does the program find his data? For that matter, how does the program determine whether Ray Buie is even in the file? Your program needs a search routine.

You could write a routine to read every record and search for the one with "Ray Buie" in it. But you would not want to have the computer **Get** and examine every record in turn, starting at 1 and continuing until it finds "Ray Buie" or reaches record 20,000, whichever comes first. This would be take too much time. Instead, you could use an *index file*, a sequential file that holds just the names of your friends, and the record number in the FRIENDS.RND file that contains each person's data.

Here's how this scenario works. When your program starts, it reads index file FRIENDS.SEQ into the computer's memory. The names go into a string array called `Friend$()`, and the record numbers into integer array `RecNum()`. Suppose that `Friend$(1)` is Aila Abbot. Aila's data is not necessarily stored in record 1 of the FRIENDS.RND file (unless the record happens to have been the first data that you entered). Suppose that Aila's name, address, phone number, and birthday happen to be in record 5. If so, `RecNum(1)` would equal 5.

Therefore, to find Greg Sora's address, you first must find Greg's position in the `Friend$()` array:

```
match = 0
For i = 1 To NumFriends
   If Friend$(i) = target$ Then      'in this case ⇒
      target$ is "Greg Sora"
      match = i
      i = NumFriends             'set i to maximum to ⇒
        get out of loop fast
   End If
Next i
```

```
If match = 0 then
    announce that target is not there
Else
    open FRIENDS.RND and Get record match
End If
```

PA2.2 Using a random access file

Suppose that NumFriends is the number of people in the your file. That is, your Friend$() array goes from Friend$(1) to Friend$(NumFriends). Thus the number of active records in the FRIENDS.RND random access data base equals NumFriends. For simplicity, assume that the FRIENDS.RND exactly matches the Friend$(1) array, so that if, for example, Friend$(1) = "Aila Abbot," RecNum(1) equals 1 and you look in record 1 of the data file. Suppose that you are using a type variable called Person that holds all the person's data. Person would have the fields Person.Name, Person.Address, Person.Phone, and Person.Birthday.

Adding a record

If you want to add a new friend to your files, you follow this procedure:

1. Increase NumFriends:

```
NumFriends = NumFriends + 1
```

2. Add the new person to the Friend$() array:

```
Friend$(NumFriends) = NewName$
```

3. Assign a new record number:

```
RecNum(NumFriends) = NumFriends
```

4. Save the changed sequential array:

```
Open "FRIENDS.SEQ" For Output as #1
        print #1, "NumFriends"
        For i = 1 to NumFriends
                Print #1, Friend$(i)
                Print #1, RecNum(i)
        Next i
Close #1
```

5. Store your friend's data in the data file (assuming the record length 200):

```
Open "FRIENDS.RND" For Random As #1 L = 200
        Put #1, NumFriends
Close #1
```

Sorting the file

Would `Friend$(x)` always be stored in record x? Not necessarily. If you sort the `Friend$()` array, the positions in the array change. But the record numbers in the random access file stay the same. That's why you used a `RecNum()` array in the first place.

After comparing `Friend$(i)` to `Friend$(j)`, your usual sort routine decides whether to swap them. In this case, if the routine decides to swap `Friend$(i)` and `Friend$(j)`, it should also swap `RecNum(i)` and `RecNum(j)` at the same time. After the sort, write the new, changed sequential file FRIENDS.SEQ to disk again.

Deleting from the file

Does the number of occupied records in FRIENDS.RND always equal `NumFriends`? That is, if `NumFriends` equals 10, are your 10 friends always stored in records 1 to 10, even if not necessarily in that order? The answer depends on how you set up your files.

In the following simple delete routine, the next available record is equal to `NumFriends + 1`, so that you can use the add routine discussed earlier. Suppose that you want to delete `Friend$(x)`. One way to do this is as follows:

1. Move the last person's data into position x:

```
Friend$(x) = Friend$(NumFriends)
RecNum(x) = RecNum(NumFriends)
```

2. Write the changed `Friend$()` and `RecNum()` arrays to the sequential file.

3. Read in record `NumFriends` from the FRIENDS.RND array:

```
Get #1, x, Person
```

4. Write the data to record x:

```
Put #1, x, Person
```

5. Decrease `NumFriends`:

```
NumFriends = NumFriends - 1
```

Notice that one friend's data is in the random file twice. The program wrote the last record over the deleted record. The last record's data is still there, but you will overwrite it as soon as you add a new person's data.

A somewhat safer way of deleting is simply to remove the person from the sequential file (steps 1 and 2) and leave the random access file alone. The data for the deleted record remains, but will be in a now unused record, because no `RecNum()` will point to it. An advantage of this method is that you can recover the deleted information if it has not been overwritten.

When you add a person, you can scan through the `RecNum()` array to find an unused value and then store the new data in *that* record.

Another method is to keep track of the number of used records. The number initially is the same as `NumFriends`, and remains equal to `NumFriends` until you delete a person's data. The program adds a new friend's data to the record `NumUsedRecords + 1`. An advantage of this method is that you can recover all data because the program doesn't overwrite any data. The disadvantage for a constantly changing list of friends is that the data file could become quite large, even if the number of friends stays fairly constant.

Application PA2 Expense Tracker

Learning Objectives

- writing and reading sequential files
- using random access files
- using InputBox$
- enabling and disabling buttons
- making controls visible and invisible
- using frames
- using Type to define variables
- using On Error GoTo for error checking
- using DateSerial
- using Printer.Print and PrintForm
- formatting for dates and currency
- building a scroll bar and a date-entry routine
- using multiple forms
- using KeyPress to monitor keystrokes (and modify appearances on the screen)
- using list boxes

Overview

The user enters expense payments, assigning each to an expense category chosen from a list. The computer saves the information on each transaction for future use and outputs it to the screen and the printer in several formats. The user can erase the transaction files after entering a password.

Figure PA2.1 shows the main form. It lists all expense totals. The user is about to enter a transaction.

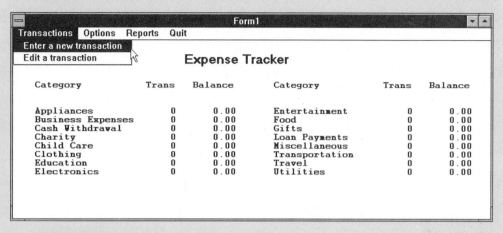

Figure PA2-1
The form before any entries

A transaction entry frame opens, as shown in Figure PA2-2. The user can use a scroll bar to set the date. A combo box on the right drops down to display the expense categories.

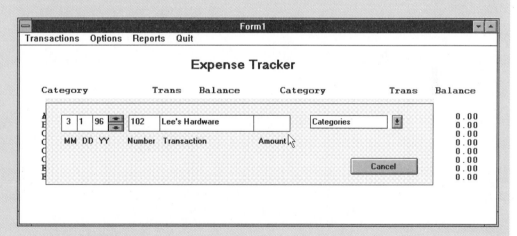

Figure PA2-2
The user is entering a transaction

Instructions

This application uses three forms and a global module. Open the File menu and choose New Module. The project window shows Module1.bas. Save it as EXPENSE.BAS. Click on your form, or select it in the project window. Save the form as EXPENSE1.FRM. Open the File menu and choose New Form, then

rename and save your form as EXPENSE2.FRM. Repeat this process and save
the third form as Password.Frm. Your project windows should show the three
form files and the basic module.

Go to the global module (**Expense.Bas**) code section and enter these definitions:

```
Type Transaction
    transdate As Double
    transnumber As Integer
    transmessage As String * 30
    transamount As Currency
    transcategory As Integer
End Type

'use these for the password frame
Global trypass As String
Global pass As Integer

Global Cat(20)  As String
Global CategoryBalance(20) As Currency
Global CategoryNumber(20) As Integer
Global LastCategory As Integer
Global NumberOfEntries As Integer
Global chosen As Integer
Global TransactionInfo(100, 2) As Integer

'TransactionInfo(i,0) is the record containing the ith ⇒
    transaction
'TransactionInfo(i,1) is the amount for that ⇒
    transaction * 100 (to⇒make it an integer)
'TransactionInfo(i,2) is the category number
```

The first lines define a type of variable as Transaction, which consists of five
fields. Later, when you define any other variable as a Transaction variable, that
variable has a similar structure.

The lines dealing with `pass` and `trypass` are used in the Password form. When
you use the password module in a future application, you need only add these
two lines to the global module.

You set up a two-dimensional array called `TransactionInfo()` to hold 100
transactions (101 actually, because you could start counting at zero). For each of
these transactions, you store three numbers. The last three lines are just messages to
you, the programmer, reminding you what the "fields" of `TransactionInfo()`
array stand for.

Now start setting up the first form, EXPENSE1.FRM, as shown in Figure PA2-3.

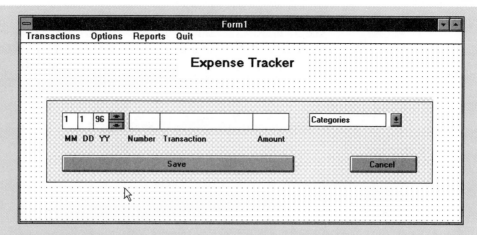

Figure PA2-3
The first form, EXPENSE1.FRM

Place the TitleBox label and then place a frame in the center of the form.
Remove the frame's caption. From left to right in the frame, place the following:

Control	Name	Caption or Text
Text box	Month1	1
Text box	Day1	1
Text box	Year1	96
Vertical scroll bar	DateScroll	
Text box	NumberBox	
Text box	TransactionBox	
Text box	AmountBox	
Combo box	category	Categories
Label	headings	(See the following text)
Button	SaveButton	Save
Button	CancelButton	Cancel

The label stretches across the frame beneath the text boxes. All the headings are
in that one label's caption:

```
MM DD YY    Number   Transaction         Amount
```

To align the headings correctly, you have to experiment with the spacing.

Select the combo box and make its Sorted property **True**.

Select the frame and make its Visible property **False**, so that it is hidden when the
form first loads. Then choose Color Palette from the Window menu and set the
frame's and label's background colors to an attractive scheme. Only some of the
colors work well as BackColors, because some colors look different behind text
from elsewhere in the frame. Try light cyan (&H00FFFFFF&) as the BackColor.

Now create the form's menu structure. While viewing the form, display the Menu Design window. Figure PA2-4 shows the menu structure. Leave the Index box blank, except for the highlighted category1. The control names are TransactionChoice, EnterChoice, EditChoice, OptionChoice, ClearChoice, ReportsChoice, DetailsChoice, CategoryChoice, PrintChoice, and QuitChoice.

Figure PA2-4
The EXPENSE1 form's menu

The form has some general declarations:

```
Dim Shared trans As Transaction
Dim whichwaslast As Integer
Dim newone As Integer
Dim r%
Dim ThisRecordCategory As Integer
Dim ThisRecordAmount As Currency
```

Now begin coding the text boxes. The first three boxes and the scroll bar must work together to enable the user to set the date. Therefore, you must tell the scroll bar which of the boxes (Month1, Day1, or Year1) it is controlling. You do that by setting a variable, called `whichwaslast`, depending on which one got the focus (by a click, a tab, or a key press). Start with Month1. Note that the following goes into GotFocus, not into Click or Change:

```
Sub Month1_GotFocus ()
    whichwaslast = 1              '1 = day selected
    Month1.ForeColor = QBColor(0)    'restore text to fi
      black
    Day1.ForeColor = QBColor(1)  'change text colour
    Year1.ForeColor = QBColor(0) 'restore text to black
    temp = Val(Day1.Text)        'remember the setting
```

```
         DateScroll.Max = 1: DateScroll.Min =12   'scroll bar ⇒
            settings
         DateScroll.Value = temp            'set scroll bar to ⇒
            saved date
      End Sub
```

The easiest way to supply code for Month1_GotFocus and Year1_GotFocus is to copy the preceding code and paste it into the others. Then change the lines involving whichwaslast, temp, and the DateScroll settings:

```
Sub Day1_GotFocus ()
   whichwaslast = 2
   Month1.ForeColor = QBColor(0)
   Day1.ForeColor = QBColor(1)         'this one blue
   Year1.ForeColor = QBColor(0)
   temp = Val(Month1.Text)
   DateScroll.Max = 1: DateScroll.Min = 31 ⇒
      'month numbers
   DateScroll.Value = temp
End Sub

Sub Year1_GotFocus ()
   whichwaslast = 3
   Day1.ForeColor = QBColor(0)
   Month1.ForeColor = QBColor(0)
   Year1.ForeColor = QBColor(1)        ''this one blue
   temp = Val(Year1.Text)
   DateScroll.Max = 96: DateScroll.Min = 99        'year ⇒
      numbers
   DateScroll.Value = temp
End Sub
```

CAREFUL: Note that the maximum values are less than the minimum values. You might recall that Visual Basic's creators decided that vertical scroll bars should increase from the top down, not from the bottom up.

The scroll bar must first set its own value when it gets the focus. Then, when the scroll bar's value changes, alter the appropriate text box, depending on the value of whichwaslast:

```
Sub DateScroll_GotFocus ()
   Select Case whichwaslast
      Case 1
         DateScroll.Value = Val(Month1.Text)
      Case 2
         DateScroll.Value = Val(Day1.Text)
      Case 3
         DateScroll.Value = Val(Year1.Text)
      Case Else
```

```
        End Select
End Sub

Sub DateScroll_Change ()
    Select Case whichwaslast
        Case 1
            Month1.Text = Str$(DateScroll.Value)
        Case 2
            Day1.Text = Str$(DateScroll.Value)

        Case 3
            Year1.Text = Str$(DateScroll.Value)
        Case Else
    End Select
End Sub
```

You are going to do something clever with the SaveButton. Until there is a valid translation, the form does not display the button. It becomes visible only after the user changes the information in one of the boxes, if the user enters a nonzero amount and has selected an expense category:

```
Sub NumberBox_Change()
    ShowSaveButton
End Sub

Sub TransactionBox_Change()
    ShowSaveButton
End Sub

Sub AmountBox_Change()
    ShowSaveButton
End Sub

Sub Category_Change()
    ShowSaveButton
End Sub

Sub Category_Click()
    ShowSaveButton
End Sub
```

Each of these refers to a named procedure.

As you know, these go in the general declarations. But did you know you don't have to switch to the general declarations first? Just type **Sub ShowSaveButton** *and Visual Basic sets up Sub ShowSaveButton, ready for you to enter the routine. Here it is:*

```
Sub ShowSaveButton ()
    If AmountBox.Text <> "" Then
        If Category.listindex <> -1 Then
            SaveButton.visible = -1
        Else
            SaveButton.visible = 0
        End If
    Else
        SaveButton.visible = 0
    End If
End Sub
```

While you are in the general declarations, you might as well enter the other named **Sub**s:

```
Sub getarecord (r%)
    Open "expense.rnd" For Random As #1 Len = Len(trans)
        Get #1, r%, trans
    Close #1


    'remember old values for edit routine
    ThisRecordCategory = trans.transcategory
    ThisRecordAmount = trans.transamount
    'fill the boxes
    NumberBox.Text = Str$(trans.transnumber)
    TransactionBox.Text = trans.transmessage
    AmountBox.Text = Str$(trans.transamount)
    'category.Text = category.List(trans.transcategory)
    Category.listindex = trans.transcategory
    Month1.Text = Format$(trans.transdate, "mm")
    Day1.Text = Format$(trans.transdate, "dd")
    Year1.Text = Format$(trans.transdate, "yy")
End Sub


Sub writerecord (r%)
    Open "expense.rnd" For Random As #1 Len = Len(trans)
        Put #1, r%, trans
    Close #1
End Sub
```

The preceding routines are for reading and writing to a random access file that holds the date, number, message, amount, and category number for each transaction entered. The read routine also fills the text boxes with the information read from the file.

The sequential file holds the number of entries and, for each transaction, some information: the category, the amount, and which record in the random access file holds the rest of the information. The file also holds some summary information: the category balances and number of items in each category.

```
Sub ReadSequentialFile ()
    Open "expense.seq" For Input As #1
        Input #1, NumberOfEntries
        For i = 1 To NumberOfEntries
            For j = 0 To 2
            Input #1, TransactionInfo(i, j)
            Next j
        Next i

        For i = 0 To categories
            Input #1, CategoryBalance(i)
            Input #1, CategoryNumber(i)
        Next i
    Close #1
End Sub




Sub writesequentialfile ()
    Open "expense.seq" For Output As #1
        Print #1, NumberOfEntries
        For i = 1 To NumberOfEntries
            For j = 0 To 2
                Print #1, TransactionInfo(i, j)
            Next j
        Next i

        For i = 0 To categories
            Print #1, CategoryBalance(i)
            Print #1, CategoryNumber(i)
        Next i
    Close #1
End Sub
```

The sequential file and the random access file include much redundancy. The transaction amounts are in both files. When you examine the rest of the code, you'll see that the record number in the random access file always matches the index. That is, the first transaction that the user enters gets stored in record 1, the second goes into record 2, and so on. But consider a different application in which you are storing names and addresses. You might have the names and record numbers in your sequential array, called an index array, and the full data for each person in the random access file. Later you might want to sort your index array in alphabetical order. You would use a new sequential file (that is, a different order in the TransactionInfo( ) array) but the random access file would stay the same. The likely result is that the data for the first name in the array might not be in record 1 of the random access file.

Also, if the user deletes some names, again the number or position of a person's name in the index array might not match the location of the rest of the data in the random access file, depending on the method that you use to perform the deletion.

Finally, a good reason for the redundancy is to provide a way to recover the data in case the index file is destroyed. Returning to the example of the names and addresses, suppose that you store the names in both files. If the sequential file is erased or corrupted (most likely by a programmer's error!), you could reconstitute it from the random access file.

The drawback of redundancy is that it sacrifices disk storage space, but the advantage is safety and speed. In this application, you print balances for each transaction category. You could find the balance for your first category, for example, by reading the entire random access file record by record and adding all the amounts that pertain to category 1. But if you instead store the totals in your sequential file, which the computer reads into memory when the program begins, the balances are instantly available. As soon as any of the data changes, you can quickly write the sequential file to disk so that it is always current.

As the preceding note mentions, when your program first starts you must read the sequential file. You could put that instruction in Form_Load, along with declarations of any variables:

```
Sub Form_Load ()
    Expense1.width = 11200: Expense1.left = 500
    LastCategory = 16 - 1    '0 to 15
    newone = 0

'fill the Category list box with the choices
    Category.AddItem "Food"
    Category.AddItem "Clothing"
    Category.AddItem "Utilities"
    Category.AddItem "Entertainment"
    Category.AddItem "Education"
    Category.AddItem "Transportation"
    Category.AddItem "Travel"
    Category.AddItem "Gifts"
    Category.AddItem "Appliances"
    Category.AddItem "Business Expenses"
    Category.AddItem "Child Care"
    Category.AddItem "Electronics"
    Category.AddItem "Loan Payments"
    Category.AddItem "Charity"
    Category.AddItem "Cash Withdrawal"
    Category.AddItem "Miscellaneous"

'add extra menu choices
    ' loop starts from 1 since CategoryChoice(0) was
    '  put there during menu creation
        For i = 1 To LastCategory
            Load CategoryChoice(i)
        Next i
```

```
'fill the cat(i) array and CategoryChoice(i) captions
   For i = 0 To LastCategory
      cat(i) = Category.List(i)
      CategoryChoice(i).Caption = cat(i)
   Next i
'So category names are in three places: the combo box, ⇒
  the cat() array
'and the pulldown menu.

'Set up the TransactonInfo() array
'fill with -1 to designate unused array values...
'(because 0 is a valid value in later code)
   For i = 0 To 100
      For j = 0 To 2
         TransactionInfo(i, j) = -1
      Next j
   Next i

   On Error GoTo nofilethere      'for first time use
   ReadSequentialFile
   On Error GoTo 0        'kill error trapping, so a
                     'different error doesn't bring us here!
Exit Sub

nofilethere:
   Close #1
   writesequentialfile
   On Error GoTo 0
Resume     'try to read the file again

End Sub
```

The form looks quite different when the program runs. The frame is invisible, and the names and balances in each transaction category are displayed. You print them to the screen. This is similar to what you would do in QBasic, except that you replace the locate command with the **CurrentX** and **CurrentY** command, which both deal with Visual Basic screen coordinates rather than columns and rows. As you did for the Invoice application in Programming Adventure 1, you change the font to Courier, a font with each letter occupying the same width. This font makes it easy to align decimal points in tables of numbers.

```
Sub Form_Paint ()
   Expense1.Cls
   Expense1.FontName = "Courier": Expense1.FontSize ⇒
      = 10
   y = 900
   Currenty = y
```

```
          Currentx = 500: Print "Category              Trans ⇒
            Balance"; 'semicolon: stay on same line
          Currentx = 6000: Print "Category         Trans ⇒
            Balance"
          Print : Print    'leave 2 blank lines
          y = Currenty          'remember where you are now
          For i = 0 To 7
             Currentx = 500: Print cat(i);
             Currentx = 3500: Print CategoryNumber(i);
             a$ = Str$(Int(CategoryBalance(i)))    'see ⇒
               what's before the decimal point
             Print Space$(7 - Len(a$));  'print enough spaces
             Print Format$(CategoryBalance(i), "#####0.00")
          Next i
          Currenty = y          'back up to where you were
          For i = 8 To 15
             Currentx = 6000: Print cat(i);
             Currentx = 9000: Print CategoryNumber(i);
             a$ = Str$(Int(CategoryBalance(i)))
             Print Space$(7 - Len(a$));
             Print Format$(CategoryBalance(i), "#####0.00")
          Next i
          Expense1.FontName = "Helv": Expense1.FontSize = 8.25
            'restore font
    End Sub
```

The preceding code shows a method for aligning the decimal places. a$ contains the characters that would appear in front of the decimal. By first printing enough spaces, depending on the length of a$, this method ensures that the decimals are always placed in the same column.

Here is the code for the other controls on the Expense1 form:

```
    Sub Cancelbutton_Click ()
       NumberBox.Text = ""
       TransactionBox.Text = ""
       AmountBox.Text = ""
       frame1.Enabled = 0 : frame1.Visible = 0
       Category.ListIndex = -1     'unselect an item
       Savebutton.Caption = "Save"   'ready for next use
    End Sub


    Sub EditChoice_Click ()
       r% = Val(InputBox$("Edit which transaction?", ⇒
         "Retrieve"))
       If r% <= NumberOfEntries And r% > 0 Then
          getarecord r%
          newone = 0                   'an existing one
          frame1.Visible = True     'bring up the ⇒
            transaction frame
          frame1.Enabled = True
```

```
               End If
               Savebutton.Caption = "Save"
         End Sub



    Sub EnterChoice_Click ()
         newone = 1                'new transaction
         Savebutton.Caption = "Save"
         Savebutton.Visible = 0   'nothing to save anymore
         frame1.Visible = -1 :frame1.Enabled = -1
    End Sub



    Sub PrintChoice_Click ()
         TotalAmount = 0
         Printer.Print "   Category"; Tab(35); ⇒
            "Transactions";⇒ Tab(52); "Balance"
         Printer.Print : Printer.Print  'leave 2 blank lines
         For i = 0 To 15
            Printer.Print "          "; cat(i);
            Printer.Print Tab(40); CategoryNumber(i);
            a$ = Str$(Int(CategoryBalance(i)))    'see ⇒
               what's before the decimal point
            Printer.Print Tab(49); "$"; Space$(7 - Len(a$));⇒
               'enough spaces
            Printer.Print Format$(CategoryBalance(i), ⇒
               "#####0.00")
            TotalAmount = TotalAmount + CategoryBalance(i)
         Next i
         Printer.Print Tab(48); "-----------"
         a$ = Str$(Int(TotalAmount))
         Printer.Print Tab(47); "$"; Space$(9 - Len(a$)); ⇒
            'print enough spaces
         Printer.Print Format$(TotalAmount, "#######0.00")
    Exit Sub

    ErrorHandler:
         Msg$ = "The form could not be printed. "
         MsgBox Msg$ ' Display message.


    End Sub



    Sub QuitChoice_Click ()
         End
    End Sub
```

SaveButton_Click does a lot. First it copies the data from the text boxes into the Transaction type variable in preparation for writing it to the disk. It uses newone to decide whether the transaction goes into a new record or the same one from which it was read when the user selected the Edit a Transaction option from the Transactions menu. Finally, it updates the balances and `TransactionInfo( )` arrays, and writes the new or changed data to disk. Here is the code:

```
Sub SaveButton_Click ()
    If Savebutton.Caption = "Save" Then
        'fill the trans variable from the text boxes
        trans.transdate = DateSerial(Val(Year1.Text), ⇒
          Val(Month1.Text), Val(Day1.Text))
        trans.transnumber = Val(NumberBox.Text)
        trans.transmessage = Left$(TransactionBox.Text,30)
        trans.transamount = Int(Val(AmountBox.Text) ⇒
          * 100 + .5) / 100
        AmountBox.Text = Str$(trans.transamount)
        trans.transcategory = Category.listindex

        If newone = 1 Then
            NumberOfEntries = NumberOfEntries + 1
            r% = NumberOfEntries 'new r%
        Else
            'decrease current amounts, because they will ⇒
              be added on later
            '(maybe in a different category)
            CategoryNumber(ThisRecordCategory) = ⇒
              CategoryNumber(ThisRecordCategory) - 1
            CategoryBalance(ThisRecordCategory) = ⇒
              CategoryBalance(ThisRecordCategory) - ⇒
                ThisRecordAmount
            'r% is known already
        End If

        'update transaction info arrays
        assignedcategory = Category.listindex

        TransactionInfo(r%, 0) = r%
        TransactionInfo(r%, 1) = Val(AmountBox.Text)
        TransactionInfo(r%, 2) = assignedcategory

        'update category totals
        CategoryNumber(assignedcategory) = ⇒
        CategoryNumber(assignedcategory) + 1
        CategoryBalance(assignedcategory) = ⇒
        CategoryBalance(assignedcategory) + ⇒
          Val(AmountBox.Text)
        writerecord r%      'write to the random file
        writesequentialfile 'update sequential file
        Savebutton.Caption = "Another"
    Else
```

```
                NumberBox.Text = "": AmountBox.Text = ""
                TransactionBox.Text = ""
                Savebutton.Caption = "Save"
                Category.ListIndex = -1
                newone = 1
            End If
            Expense1.Cls: Form_Paint      'update screen stats
        End Sub
```

When the user wants to see the transactions for one category, the program checks whether any transactions exist and then displays a second form:

```
        Sub CategoryChoice_Click (index As Integer)
            totalcount = 0
            For i = 0 To NumberOfEntries
                If TransactionInfo(i, 2) = index Then
                    totalcount = totalcount + 1
                End If
            Next i
            If totalcount = 0 Then
                MsgBox "There have been no transactions for " + ⇒
                    cat(index), 0, "Transaction Details"
            Else
                chosen = index
                expense2.Show
            End If
        End Sub
```

Clearing the sequential array is fatal (although you *could* recover the data, as the previous note explained). To protect against this, you use some password protection. A new form, Password.Frm, pops up. This frame returns with a value for the variable trypass. The following code lines check whether the variable matches the unimaginative password "password." If so, the program clears the variables to zero and writes a new sequential file. Further explanations follow.

```
        Sub ClearChoice_Click ()
            pass=0: trypass = ""      '(quote-quote)
            Password.Show 1
            If LCase$(trypass) <> "password" Then Exit Sub
            'If pass <> 3970 Then Exit Sub    'use this to ⇒
                encrypt password
            NumberOfEntries = 0
            For i = 0 To LastCategory
                TransactionInfo(i, 0) = 0: TransactionInfo(i, 1)⇒
                    = 0
                TransactionInfo(i, 2) = 0
                CategoryBalance(i) = 0: CategoryNumber(i) = 0
            Next i
            writesequentialfile
            Expense1.Cls: Form_Paint
        End Sub
```

When clearing the files, you need not clear the records in the random access file. If you zero the sequential file, the first new transaction goes into record 1, replacing the old data.

The password for this routine is coded into a line in your program. Therefore, anyone who gains access to your source code (this coding, rather than the compiled .EXE program) can find the password. Clever hackers can even get the password from the .EXE file. Although a compiled program is not a text file, and cannot be loaded into word processors, hackers have disk editor programs that can display the code. Using such a program, the hacker gets a display of a set of ASCII characters that correspond to the password in what otherwise looks like gibberish in the code.

This program includes a simple encryption technique. As you will see later, the Password.Frm can return a number that corresponds to the password in the main program. The number for "password" is 1370. As you will see when you examine the code, the number consists of the sum of the ASCII values for each character in the password times its position. (For example, "abc" codes as ASC("a") times 1 + ASC("b") times 2 + ASC("c") times 3, which equals 590.) This encryption method is by no means sophisticated, but does demonstrate how you can hide the password. The lines in the preceding routine and in Password.Frm (described later) that deal with this encryption method begin with apostrophes. If you want, you can remove the preceding trypass line and use these password encryption lines instead.

You have now done most of the work. You have two more forms to make, but each is much less complex than the first form. Select Expense2.Frm and give it two labels, a list box (not a frame or text box), and two command buttons. The sizes of the form and list box are important:

Form	Left	Top	Width	Height
Expense2	1620	1695	8400	5310
List1	360	1080	7575	2295

The general declarations need only contain your transaction type variable:

```
Dim Shared trans As Transaction
```

Place into Expense2's Form_Load the commands necessary to size the form and list box.

The list is to contain the detailed information on all the transactions in one category. Therefore, each time that the program loads the form, you must (after defining the size of the form and frame to make certain that you can fit all the information for each of the transactions) follow these steps:

1. Check whether each transaction is of the chosen category

2. Get each transaction's record number from the `TransactionInfo( )` array

3. Read that record into memory

4. Print the date, message, amount, and record number

5. Total the amounts to provide a summary line

Make certain that you place the following code into Expense2.Form_Paint, not Expense1.Form_Paint:

```
Sub Form_Paint ()
    label1.Caption = "Transactions for " + cat(chosen)
    For i = 1 To NumberOfEntries
        If TransactionInfo(i, 2) = chosen Then
            r% = TransactionInfo(i, 0)
            getarecord r%
            amount$ = Format$(trans.transamount, ⇒
              "$####0.00")
            dollar$ = Space$(11 - Len(amount$)) + amount$
            num$ = Right$("     " + ⇒
              Str$(trans.transnumber), 5)
            a$ = Format$(trans.transdate, "mmm dd,yyyy ")⇒
              + num$ + " " + trans.transmessage + ⇒
                dollar$ + "     (#" + Str$(r%) + ")"
            List1.AddItem a$
        End If
    Next i
    cnt = CategoryNumber(chosen)
    amount$ = Format$(CategoryBalance(chosen), ⇒
      "$######0.00")
    dollar$ = Space$(13 - Len(amount$)) + amount$
    summary.Caption = "Totals:        " + Right$("     " ⇒
      + Str$(count), 5) + Space$(29) + dollar$
End Sub
```

You cannot place the preceding code into Form_Load, because the application loads the form only once (unless you unload it). If you put this code in Form_Load and then want to view a second category's transactions, you wouldn't see them. *(Try it for yourself. Simply copy the preceding code, paste it into Form_Load, and enter **Exit Sub** after the opening line in Form_Load. Then run the program.)*

One line in **Sub** Form_Paint is getarecord r%. You have already coded a Sub getarecord routine in the Expense1 form. But now you are coding a different form. Visual Basic looks for **Sub**s locally, in the current form's general section, unless you add the form name to the front of the **Sub**. That is, if a line of code in the Expense2 form is getarecord r%, Expense2 must have a getarecord form. If you specify Expense1.getarecord r%, the program uses the getarecord routine in Expense1.

The getarecord routine in Expense1 is longer than you need here, so make a new **Sub** getarecord in this form:

```
Sub getarecord (r%)
    Open "expense.rnd" For Random As #1 Len = Len(trans)
        Get #1, r%, trans
    Close #1
End Sub
```

The BackButton must remove all the items in the list, before changing to another transaction category.

```
Sub BackButton_Click ()
    cnt = List1.ListCount
    For i = cnt To 1 Step -1
        List1.RemoveItem i - 1
    Next i
    expense2.Hide
    Expense1.Show
End Sub
```

Finally, Expense2's PrintButton_Click( ) routine demonstrates a terrific built-in Visual Basic routine, **PrintForm**. It uses an error-trapping routine, in case the printer is turned off or some other problem situation arises.

```
Sub printbutton_Click ()
    On Error GoTo ErrorHandler ' Set up error handler.
    PrintForm  ' Print form.
Exit Sub
ErrorHandler:
    Msg$ = "The form could not be printed. "
    MsgBox Msg$ ' Display message.
End Sub
```

You'll like Password.Frm. There's more to this form than meets the eye. Figure PA2-5 shows the form in action, after the user has typed four different letters of his or her password.

Figure PA2-5
The password form in action

To create the password form, open the File menu and choose New Form. Change the form's caption to that shown in Figure PA2-6. Then change the form's FontName to Symbol. Add an Okbutton and make the form's BorderStyle 1 (fixed single). Although the form's appearance doesn't noticeably change during design time, the form won't display any buttons across the top when the program is run. Finally, insert a picture box (*not a text box*).

Figure PA2-6
The picture box in the form

Then place a label inside the picture as shown in Figure PA2-7. Leave the label's BorderStyle at its default style of 0 (none). When the program runs, the label is invisible. Set the label's FontSize to 24.

Figure PA2-7
A label inside the picture

Define the variable `crsr` in the general declarations:

```
Dim Crsr As String
```

In Form_Load, set the Password.Left and Password.Top so that the form is centered within the screen:

```
Sub Form_Load ()
    password.Left = (Screen.Width - password.Width) / 2
    password.Top = (Screen.Height - password.Height) / 2
End Sub
```

When the password form appears, the user is to enter a password. The letters are not to show on the screen. You must ensure that when the form appears, the OKbutton has the focus and thus intercepts key presses. For each character pressed, the label box displays an asterisk. If the user presses Enter, the OKbutton_Click routine takes over.

When the user presses a key, the program executes the KeyPress routine in the active control (the one that has the focus). To ensure that the OKbutton has the focus, you set OKbutton's TabIndex to 0. For this reason, you place in OKbutton_KeyPress the routine to monitor and collect keystrokes and display asterisks:

```
Sub OKbutton_KeyPress (KeyAscii As Integer)
    Static Cnt As Integer
    If KeyAscii = 8 Then    'Backspace was pressed
        If Len(trypass) Then
```

```
                trypass = Left$(trypass, Len(trypass) - 1) ⇒
                    'remove last key
            End If
        Else
            If Len(trypass) = 0 Then
                trypass = Chr$(KeyAscii)
            Else
                trypass = trypass + Chr$(KeyAscii)
            End If
        End If
        'Update the displayed asterisks
        label1.Caption = String$(Len(trypass), "*") + Curs
End Sub
```

Finally, add the code for **OKbutton_Click**:

```
Sub OKbutton_Click ()
    If Right$(trypass, 1) <> " " Then       '(" space ")
        'For the following simple encryption method, ⇒
            remove apostrophes
        'pass = 0
        'For i = 1 To Len(trypass)
        '   pass = pass + i * Asc(Mid$(LCase$(trypass), ⇒
          i, 1))
        'Next i
        'trypass has been encrypted into pass, an integer

        Unload password
    End If
End Sub
```

As discussed previously, the simple encryption routine shown in the preceding code keeps adding a number to the variable `pass` that is equal to the ASCII value of the each letter in the password times the position in which it occurs. If you decide to try the password encryption technique, remember to enable it in the main form's Sub ClearChoice_Click ( ). After collecting the password, the form unloads, disappearing from the screen.

Modifications

1. Before printing occurs, display a message box that announces that printing is about to begin and that enables the user to click on **OK** or **Cancel**.

2. The Expense2 form could use some headings across the top, to announce that the columns are transaction number, date, message, and record number. Incidentally, the transaction numbers need not start at one. They could be, for example, the numbers of the checks used to pay the expenses.

3. The program allows room for 20 categories. Think up a few more and add them.

Enhancements

1. The name and location of the data files used for this application are fixed. Add a common dialog box control to enable the user to select the name for the data files. This addition should also enable the user to load different files for each month or for different bank accounts.

2. To use this application to keep track of the bank account balance, you can add buttons for Deposit or Withdrawal.

Chapter 13 Using Timers and Pictures

Sometimes your application might need a timer. You might decide to place a pause in some routine and then have the routine continue without user interaction. Or you might want a message to appear after a certain period of time. Or perhaps you want to display a running clock in the upper corner of the screen. In this chapter, you learn how to accomplish these tasks. As you read, enter the demonstration routines on the computer.

13.1 Using the timer control

Visual Basic is driven by events, by the actions that the user takes on your controls. To this point, you have placed the code for any program activity into **Sub**s that are triggered by user actions. In every application so far, if the user does nothing, the program does nothing. Until the user click on a button, slides a scroll bar, or presses a key, the program just sits there.

But what if you want something to happen even if the user does nothing? In almost every computer arcade game, things happen "by themselves": the enemy comes toward you, the plane keeps flying, a message pops up on the screen. Timers are used to cause the program to execute some code while waiting for user action. They are also used to delay or pause some routine, and then restart it automatically.

The timer control's important properties are Interval, the number of milliseconds (thousandths of a second) before the timer routine executes, and Enabled, which turns the timer on. Here's how the timer works. When you set Enabled to **True**, the program starts counting milliseconds. When it reaches the time specified by the Interval property, the program starts executing the code in the time's **Sub**.

To see a simple timer in action, create the form shown in Figure 13-1.

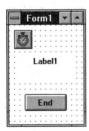

Figure 13-1
A timer demonstration form

The location of the timer control isn't important, because it will not be visible on the form when the program runs. Set the timer's Enabled property to True. Set the timer's Interval to 1,000.

Click on the timer and add these statements:

```
Sub Timer1_Timer ()
   If Label1.Caption = "" Then
     Label1.Caption = "Working"
   Else
     Label1.Caption = ""
   End If
End Sub
```

Code your EndButton and clear Label1's caption. Then run the program. Label1's caption should flash on and off in one-second (1,000 millisecond) intervals.

How could you make the word "Working" flash off and on at half-second intervals?

How could you make the length of the "off" period a half second while the length of the "on" period a full second? (One way is to add two lines to the Timer1_Timer code. Another is to use two timers. Later in this chapter, you see an application that uses several timers.)

Try this modification. Change Timer1's Enabled property to **False**. The design time setting of the Enabled property determines whether the timer is in countdown mode when the program first starts. Reduce its Interval to 100. Then add a Go button, as shown in Figure 13-2.

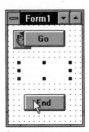

Figure 13-2
Add a Go button

Here is the new button's code:

```
Sub Go_Click ()
   If Go.Caption = "Go" Then    'clock is stopped; so ...
     Timer1.Enabled = True        'start it
     Go.Caption = "Stop"          'change caption
     Label1.Caption = ""          'wipe label1
   Else                           'clock is running; so ...
     Timer1.Enabled = False       'stop it
     Go.Caption = "Go"            'change caption
   End If
End Sub
```

Notice that this code checks the control's own caption to decide what to do.

13.2 Displaying the time and date

Visual Basic has three built-in functions for time keeping: **Date$**, **Time$**, and **Timer**. The function **Date$** displays the date in mm-dd-yyyy format.[1] **Time$** gives you an expression for the current time. To see these functions in operation, modify the timer program by changing **Sub** Timer1_Timer as follows:

```
Sub Timer1_Timer ()
    Lf$ = Chr$(10) + Chr$(13)
    Label1.Caption = Time$ & Lf$ & Date$
End Sub
```

Chr$(10) and **Chr$(13)** are line feed and carriage return respectively. Use them between strings that you are joining, to make the second string appear on the next line (regardless of the label box's width). Figure 13-3 shows the running program.

Figure 13-3
Adding the date and time

Timer is a value equal to the number of seconds that have elapsed since midnight. Like **Rnd**'s value, **Timer**'s value is always changing.

If you want to place a timed pause in the middle of a routine, you can use a **Timer** statement. For example, the following code creates a three-second pause:

```
Sub SomethingOrOther
    .... 'sub does something initially

    T = Timer    'read the clock. T holds Timer's ⇒
      current value
    Do Until Timer > T + 3
    Loop   'Cycle until Timer is 3 s more than its ⇒
      original value

    ... 'sub continues after three-second pause
End Sub
```

---

[1] The format depends on the options that you set the International dialog box, which you display by opening the Main menu, choosing Control Panel, and selecting International. In that dialog box, you can change (or may have already changed) the display format to *dd-mm-yyyy* or some other format of your choice.

Timer is a function. Don't confuse it with the timer control. You use **Timer** to count seconds from the system clock. The preceding example stores the current value of **Timer** in variable T. Then the program sits in a loop until **Timer** (always increasing) is three seconds more than T, **Timer**'s original value.

Here's how to use **Timer** to change the small program that you have been developing into a stop watch simulation. First define the global variable T in the general declarations:

```
Dim T As Single
```

Add one line to Go button's Click routine to read the value of **Timer** into T. Here is the entire routine, but you need only add the single line near the middle:

```
Sub Go_Click ()
   If Go.Caption = "Go" Then   'clock is stopped; so ...
      Timer1.Enabled = True    'start it
      Go.Caption = "Stop"      'change caption
      Label1.Caption = ""      'wipe label1
      T = Timer                'read the timer <<<<<< ⇒
         the only new line

   Else                        'clock is running; so ...
     Timer1.Enabled = False    'stop it
     Go.Caption = "Go"         'change caption
   End If
End Sub
```

Change the Label1.Caption line in **Sub** Timer1_Timer so that the program displays the number of seconds that have passed since the value of T was set:

```
Sub Timer1_Timer ()
Lf$ = Chr$(10) + Chr$(13)
Label1.Caption = Time$ & Lf$ & Date$ & Lf$ & ⇒
  Format$(Timer - T, ⇒ "##0.00")
End Sub
```

When the user clicks on the Go button, the watch starts. T is a variable that holds the value of **Timer** when the user starts the watch by clicking on the Go button. Therefore, **Timer** minus T is the number of seconds since that time.

Every time that you click on the Go button, the stop watch begins at zero. An improvement to this scheme is to create another button that does not stop the clock but displays the elapsed time in a different window. This enhancement would be useful for showing a runner's time at the halfway point of a race. Of course, you would not need to show the date and time anymore.

13.3 Displaying pictures in your application

The picture box control enables you to place a picture in the form. The picture can be an icon (.ICO file) or a bitmap (.BMP).[2] You can draw a picture in the Paintbrush program and save it as a .BMP file or use one of the many file converter programs to convert to .BMP format a .GIF picture that you might have downloaded from a bulletin board.

You can add the picture to your application at design time or run time. To place a picture on your form, select the picture control. Place and size the box that is to contain the graphic. The default name is Picture1. Then choose the Picture property. The property's initial setting is (none), but a click on ▣ at the top of the properties box brings up a file open dialog box in which you can search for a picture.

If you know where a file will be on your user's computer, you can load into a picture box a picture called Picture1 at run time rather than at design time:

```
Picture1.Picture = LoadPicture(C:\WINDOWS\LEAVES.BMP)
```

This works only if the file LEAVES.BMP is in the C:\WINDOWS directory.

To see how to use LoadPicture and how to deal with a missing picture, try creating the small demonstration program shown in Figure 13-4.

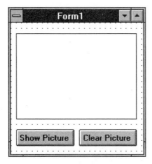

Figure 13-4
Using the picture control

The form has two buttons and a picture. There are two small **Sub**s:

```
Sub ShowButton_Load ()
  On Error Resume Next
  Picture1.Picture = ⇒
    LoadPicture("C:\windows\leaves.bmp")
  If Err Then
    MsgBox "Could not find the picture"
  End If
End Sub
```

---

[2]Two other, more obscure Windows picture file formats are available: a run-length encode file (.RLE) or a metafile (.WMF).

```
Sub ClearButton_Click ()
   Picture1.Picture = LoadPicture()
End Sub
```

If you have LEAVES.BMP in a C:\WINDOWS directory (the picture comes with Windows), you should see the picture. If not, `Err` becomes nonzero, the program resumes at the line after the one that caused the error, and a message box appears.

Notice how you use **LoadPicture( )** to remove the picture from the box without removing the box itself.

Try this modification: Add a common dialog open file box so that when the user clicks on the Show Picture button, he or she can select the picture.

The form itself can hold a picture. In the form shown in Figure 13-5, you can delete the picture box and replace Picture1 with Form1 in the two **Sub**s. Then you see the picture appear as a background to any controls on the form.

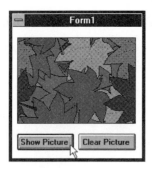

Figure 13-5
The running form

Application 13 Creating animation with pictures and timers

Overview   The traffic lights at an intersection cycle through their changing colors. The user can control the cycle time. Simultaneously, a digital time-of-day clock ticks on. An optional routine enables the user to display the clock in analog mode (with revolving hands).

Learning Objectives
- using a scroll bar
- using **Str$** to change a number to a string
- changing a timer's interval
- using multiple timers

- using **Time$** to create a real-time clock
- loading pictures
- optional:
  - using simple graphics, such as picture frames, lines, and simple animation
  - calculating the outsides of circles
  - putting a label inside a picture
  - changing colors

Instructions

Figure 13-6 shows the form during the design stage and when running. First make the four picture boxes (not text boxes or labels) that will hold the traffic lights. Call them west, east, north, and south. Put another picture box in the center of the intersection; then, *on top of the picture box*, put a label with the control name Clock. By moving the label up or down you can center the label contents *vertically* inside a frame.

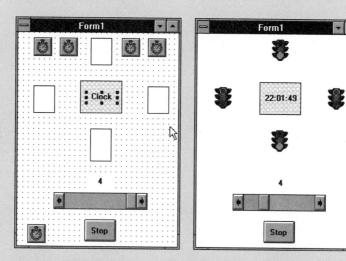

Figure 13-6
The traffic form at design time and run time

Make a Stop button. Then add five timers, a horizontal scroll bar, and a label. You can leave the default names on these items.

Set the properties for these objects:

- Set timers 1–4 to Enabled = **False** and Interval = 1000.
- Set Hscroll1.Min to 2 and Max to 10.
- Start with a 4 in Label1 under the scroll bar.
- Change all the pictures' BorderStyle to False.

● Set Clock.Alignment to 2 (centered).

● Use the color palette to set Picture1's and Clock's BackColors to any color that you want. &H00FFFFC0 works well.

Define the variables red, green, and yellow as strings in the general declarations:

```
Dim red As String
Dim green As String
Dim yellow As String
```

The traffic signal lights are icons that come with Visual Basic. You should find them on your computer, or you can copy them from the disk that accompanies this book. Put the icons' names and paths into these string variables in Form_Load:

```
Sub Form_Load ()
    green = "c:\vb\icons\traffic\trffc10a.ico"
    yellow = "c:\vb\icons\traffic\trffc10b.ico"
    red = "c:\vb\icons\traffic\trffc10c.ico"
    west.Picture = LoadPicture(red)
    east.Picture = LoadPicture(red)
    north.Picture = LoadPicture(green)
    south.Picture = LoadPicture(green)
    Timer2.Interval = 4000      '4 seconds
    Hscroll1.Value = 4          'to represent 4 seconds
    Timer2.Enabled = True
    west.BorderStyle = 0        'not needed if you set ⇒
        it to false already
    east.BorderStyle = 0
    north.BorderStyle = 0
    south.BorderStyle = 0

End Sub
```

The scroll bar controls the timer's intervals. Show its value in Label1:

```
Sub Hscroll1_Change ()
    Label1.Caption = Str$(Hscroll1.Value)
End Sub
```

To run the clock, you need to add only one line to Timer1_Timer:

```
Sub Timer5_Timer ()
    clock.Caption = Time$
End Sub
```

Now code the four timers. Timer1's job is to set Timer2 for the interval determined by the scroll bar, then display north and south green and east and west red. First Timer1 disables itself, loads the icon files into the pictures, then sets and turns on Timer2.

```
Sub Timer1_Timer ()
  'east west red,
  Timer1.Enabled = False
  west.Picture = LoadPicture(red)
  east.Picture = LoadPicture(red)
  north.Picture = LoadPicture(green)
  south.Picture = LoadPicture(green)
  Timer2.Interval = Val(Label1.Caption) * 1000 - 1000
  Timer2.Enabled = True
End Sub
```

When Timer2 engages, it turns itself off, makes north and south yellow, and sets Timer3 to one second (1,000 ms). Thus Timer3 engages one second later, to turn the lights red.

```
Sub Timer2_Timer ()
  Timer2.Enabled = False
  north.Picture = LoadPicture(yellow)
  south.Picture = LoadPicture(yellow)
  Timer3.Enabled = True
  Timer3.Interval = 1000
End Sub
```

Similarly, Timer3 and Timer4 complete the cycle for east and west green and then yellow:

```
Sub Timer3_Timer ()
  'east west green, store time of cycle in Timer4
  Timer3.Enabled = False
  west.Picture = LoadPicture(green)
  east.Picture = LoadPicture(green)
  north.Picture = LoadPicture(red)
  south.Picture = LoadPicture(red)
  Timer4.Interval = Val(Label1.Caption) * 1000 - 1000
  Timer4.Enabled = True
End Sub
```

```
Sub Timer4_Timer ()
  'east and west were green, show yellow
  Timer4.Enabled = False
  west.Picture = LoadPicture(yellow)
  east.Picture = LoadPicture(yellow)
  Timer1.Interval = 1000
  Timer1.Enabled = True
End Sub
```

Run the program and watch as the clock keeps ticking while the lights change and as you adjust the scroll bar. This application demonstrates how Visual Basic can keep track of two independently timed cycles.

Modification

In real life, the lengths of the red and green cycles differ. For example, north and south might be red for 30 seconds but green for only 20 seconds (which means, of course, that east and west would be the opposite, neglecting the length of the yellow). Use two scroll bars, one for the number of seconds for the north and south red light and the other for the duration of the green light.

Enhancement

You might want to display an analog clock. This requires simple graphics to draw the moving hands, which require a couple dozen lines of code, including a named **Sub** procedure. The code for both types of clock is shown later in this Enhancement section. This book doesn't formally present the topic of graphics until the next chapter, but you might enjoy this preview of animation graphics.

An analog clock has hands moving in a circle. This requires trigonometry. (However, you don't have to know trigonometry to complete this enhancement; just copy the code.) You have to declare some extra variables in the general declarations. Add these lines to the three lines that are already in the general declarations:

```
'the following variables are used with the analog clock
Dim xc, yc, xs, ys, xh, yh, xm, ym, x1, y1 As Integer
Dim analog As Integer
Dim pi, s, m, h As Double
Dim twopi, halfpi As Double
Dim erasewith As Long
```

The program must give many of these variables values when it begins. An appropriate place to specify these values is in Form_Load. Add the following to the lines that you already have:

```
Sub Form_Load ()

    '... lines already there

    'add these variables for the analog clock
    pi = 3.1415926
    twopi = 2 * pi: halfpi = pi / 2
    picture1.DrawWidth = 2
    xc = Picture1.Width/2:yc = Picture1.Height/2
      'center of clock
    xs = xc: ys = yc
    xm = xc: ym = yc
    xh = xc: yh = yc
End Sub
```

Timer5 governs the clock. Although the digital clock display requires only one line, the analog clock takes more. Here is the complete Timer5_Timer routine for both clocks:

```
Sub Timer5_Timer ()
    If analog = 0 Then                        'show digital clock
        picture1.Cls                          'digital
        clock.Caption = Time$                 'digital
        clock.visible = True                  'digital
    Else                                      'analog clock
        clock.Caption = "": clock.visible = False
        h = Val(Left$(Time$, 2))              'hour
        s = Val(Right$(Time$, 2)):            'second
        m = Val(Mid$(Time$, InStr(Time$, ":") + 1, 2))
            'minute

        picture1.DrawWidth = 1
        FindOutside 350, s / 60    'named Sub to ⇒
            calculate tip of hand
        erasewith = picture1.backcolor
        If x1 <> xs Or y1 <> ys Then picture1.Line (xc,⇒
            yc)-(xs, ys), erasewith
        xs = x1: ys = y1
        picture1.Line (xc, yc)-(xs, ys), 0
                                              'minute hand
        picture1.DrawWidth = 2
        FindOutside 250, (m + s / 60) / 60
        If x1 <> xm Or y1 <> ym Then picture1.Line (xc,⇒
            yc)-(xm, ym),⇒ erasewith
        xm = x1: ym = y1
        picture1.Line (xc, yc)-(xm, ym), QBColor(1)
                                              'hour hand
        picture1.DrawWidth = 4
        FindOutside 150, (h + m / 60) / 12
        If x1 <> xh Or y1 <> yh Then picture1.Line (xc,⇒
            yc)-(xh, yh), erasewith
        xh = x1: yh = y1
        picture1.Line (xc, yc)-(xh, yh), QBColor(1)

    End If

End Sub
```

The preceding routine refers to a **Sub** that figures the location of the ends of each hand, given the radius of the hand and the number of time units (between 0 and 60) to display. Put this new **Sub** in the general declarations:

```
Sub FindOutside (r, a)
    angle! = -twopi * a + halfpi
    x1 = xc + r * Cos(angle!)
    y1 = yc - r * Sin(angle!)
End Sub
```

The clock display toggles between analog and digital when you click on the form or the clock. Add a line to Form_Click and put the same line in Picture1_Click and Clock_Click:

```
Sub Form_Click ()
    analog = 1 - analog    '1 becomes 0 or 0 becomes 1
End Sub
```

Finally, fix your Stop button. The user must click on it to end the program.

About the variables: A variable declared to be **Double** *holds a floating-point (decimal) number with twice as many digits as one declared to be* **Single,** *which tracks seven digits. The variables for the angles use* pi *(π), which is specified to eight-digit accuracy. This is why you use* **Double.** **Long** *refers to an integer that is greater than 32,767. Colors are long integers, so you declare* erasewith *to be* **Long**.

Look closely at the background of the clock as the second hand sweeps across it. Fix the problem.

A potential bug arises if the clock passes midnight. Do you see what would happen?

Exercises

At your desk

1   What property of a timer do you set to determine how much time is to elapse before the timer's **Sub** executes?

2   What setting do you use for a 10-second countdown?

3   What line of code turns on a timer?

4   What Visual Basic functions do you use to specify the date and time?

5   The C:\WINDOWS directory includes a picture called ARCADE.BMP. What command do you enter to load the picture into ARCPIC, a picture control, while the program is running?

At your computer

Make a reaction timer game. Figure 13-7 shows the form, which includes a label, option button, timer, and Begin button. When the user clicks on Begin, both buttons disappear. After a short interval, the option button becomes visible as the target. When the user clicks on the button, the program reports how long it took the user to respond, as shown in Figure 13-8.

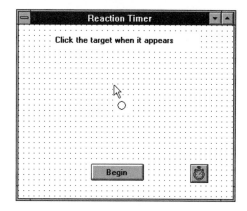

Figure 13-7
The Reaction Timer form

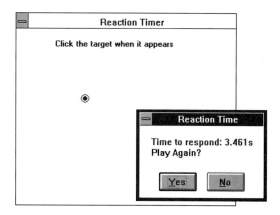

Figure 13-8
The user has clicked on the target

Leave the option button enabled at all times, but make its Visible property False when the game begins. You use the timer to cause a random pause before making the target visible. This line creates a random interval between 1 to 4 seconds:

```
Timer1.Interval = Rnd * 3000 + 1000
Timer1.Enabled = True
```

You could make this program a more enjoyable arcade-style game by having the option button move to random left and top positions. You can use the following statements to pick a random value for the top of the bull's eye:

```
'pick random top
  TopOfRange = Label1.Top + Label1.Height
  BottomOfRange = Form1.Height - Option1.Height
  Range = BottomOfRange - TopOfRange
  Option1.Top = Rnd * Range + TopOfRange
```

Follow this pattern to set Option1.Left to a random position. You should be able to decide in what Sub to place this code.

You would also want to disable the Stop button while it actually says Stop so that the user cannot use that button again. Don't forget to enable it when it says Again.

Chapter 14 Adding Your Own Graphics

You have seen how to load a previously drawn picture into a picture box on your form. Visual Basic has some commands that you can use to add simple graphics to your program. You used the **Line** statement in Programming Adventure 1 when you constructed an invoice application. In this chapter, you see how to draw some other basic shapes.

14.1 Setting the form's size and scale

Like other controls, the form has top, left, height, and width properties. Sometimes you might want to make the form's size or location different at run time than they were at design time. For example, while designing a form, you often keep it small so that you can easily use the toolbox, color palette, and properties list. At run time, you can enlarge and reposition your form by setting the conditions in Form_Load:

```
Sub Form_Load ()
    Form1.Top = 100
    Form1.height = 6000
    Form1.Left = 100
    Form1.Width = 10000
End Sub
```

These lines define a coordinate system for the form. The point (0,0) is the top-left corner and the bottom-right corner is (6000,10000). As you will see in the next section, you can draw lines between points. (Actually, you did this in Programming Adventure 1.) For example, you draw a horizontal line near the top of the form, not quite touching each side, with a statement such as the following:

```
Line (1000, 100) - (5000, 100)
```

Now suppose that when you run your program, you decide to change the width of your form. The line will not be in the same relative position unless you change the numbers in the **Line** statement. In fact, you would have to adjust all **Line** statements (and statements that position buttons and other controls). There is a better way.

No matter what the actual size of the form, you can define its inside coordinate system to be any size that you want by using the properties ScaleHeight and ScaleWidth. Include in Form_Load these statements:

```
Form1.ScaleHeight = 1000
Form1.ScaleWidth = 1000
```

The result is that, whether the form is small, thin, wide, or tall, its inside coordinate system goes from (0, 0) to (1000, 1000). If you change the size of the form during the design stage, all elements maintain their relative sizes and places.

14.2 Drawing lines, circles, and boxes

Windows is a *graphical user interface* (GUI). Before Windows, most programs that did not use graphics displayed their output on the *text screen*. (Whenever you see the DOS C:> prompt, you are looking at the text screen.) On this screen, you can display any of the 255 ASCII characters that make up the original IBM character set: letters, numbers, symbols, and some built-in graphics characters such as ⌈, =, and ⌉. The smallest object that you could place on the screen was one of these characters. Eighty would fit across the screen, and you could have 25 rows of characters.

The individual characters themselves are made of *pixels*, which correspond[1] to the dots that you can turn on or off on the screen.[2] The characters on the text screen are composed of eight dots across by 14 dots down.

Other graphics screens were available to programs. On these screens, you could control the individual pixels. Depending on the type of graphics capability that your computer had, you could display 320 pixels by 175 (in which case each pixel on the screen is large), 640 by 350 (smaller pixels), 800 by 600 (smaller still), or 1,024 by 768 (very high resolution).

Because Windows is a GUI, Visual Basic always uses graphics screens. Therefore, you have access to individual pixels and can draw on your form.

To see some of the shapes that you can draw at run time, create the form shown in Figure 14-1.

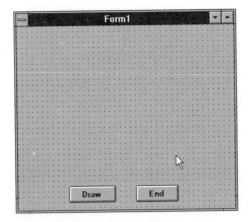

Figure 14-1
You can draw shapes on this form

---

[1]You can see the dots on your television screen if you look closely. On good quality monitors, however, the dots are so close together that you may have trouble seeing them. These dots are not actually equivalent to pixels. The size and spacing of the dots are determined by the hardware (the type of monitor that you have). The size of a pixel, one unit over which the programmer has on/off control, is determined by the program that is displaying its output on the screen. One pixel, for example, might be actually three dots wide.

[2]On digital monitors, a dot is either on or off. On analog monitors, the intensities of the dots can vary, allowing more colors.

Set the form's BackColor to &H00C0C0C0&, which is gray on the color palette. Make a pair of buttons called DrawButton and EndButton.

In Form_Load, define your form's ScaleHeight and ScaleWidth:

```
Sub Form_Load ()
    ScaleWidth = 1000
    ScaleHeight = 1000
End Sub
```

As you learned in Section 14.1, the statement `Width = 1000` gives a form the "physical" width of 1,000 when you run the program. If you specify `ScaleWidth = 1000`, the form has whatever width it had when you created it, but it has "logical" width of 1000. That is, the form's internal coordinate system will be based on a scale of 0 (left side) to 1,000 (right side.)

Enter the following code for DrawButton, run the program, and read the explanations that follow as you view the screen that you have drawn:

```
Sub DrawButton_Click ()

    'define some constants
    blue = QBColor(1): red = QBColor(4)
    brightcyan = QBColor(11): brightblue = QBColor(9)

    FillStyle = 1: FillColor = 'defaults: ⇒
       transparent/ black
    Line (5, 5)-(995, 995)         '(pixel across, pixel down)
    Line (80, 140)-(175, 280), blue, BF   'blue filled box
    Line (100, 550)-(300, 700), QBColor(14), B 'yellow box
    Line (200, 800)-(600, 900), QBColor(5), BF 'violet box

    Pset (400, 150), red                      'red dot
    Circle (400, 150), 50, QBColor(2)         'green circle

    pi = 3.1415926          'define this
    Circle (700, 250), 200, red, 0, pi, 1 / 4    'red arc
    Circle (700, 300), 200, red, , , 1 / 4       'red oval

    FillStyle = 0: FillColor = QBColor(14)        'solid,⇒
       color yellow
    Circle (600, 600), 50, , -pi / 2, -pi   'black ⇒
       wedge, filled yellow
```

```
    FillStyle = 0: FillColor = brightblue          'solid, ⇒
      bright blue
    Circle (850, 600), 130, brightblue, , , 3 / 2  'oval

    FillStyle = 7: FillColor = brightcyan 'diagonal ⇒
      grid / bright cyan
    Circle (850, 600), 100, brightcyan, , , 3 / 2 ⇒
      'inner oval

FillStyle = 1: FillColor = 0              'return to defaults

End Sub
```

You use the **Line** command to draw the following:

Lines	`Line (x1, y1) - (x2, y2), color`
	`Line -(x3, y3), color  '(from last point)`
Boxes (rectangles)	`Line (x1, y1) - (x2, y2), color, B`
Filled boxes	`Line (x1, y1) - (x2, y2), color, BF`

(x1, y1) and (x2, y2) are the end points of the line, or the diagonal of the box. If you omit the first coordinate, the program draws a line from the last plotted point. The BF for a filled box is a leftover from QBasic, the language from which Visual Basic derives. A more flexible method of filling the box with a chosen color is to use the form's FillStyle and FillColor properties.

The FillStyle property determines whether drawn boxes, circles, and ovals are solid, transparent, or patterned. You can see the list of patterns during the design phase by selecting your form, choosing the property FillStyle, and pulling down the Settings box.

You can specify colors by their hex number, which you can find by selecting a color from the color palette and checking the properties box for the number. For example, &H000000FF& is red. As Chapter 6 mentioned, you can use another remnant of the QBasic language, QBColor, to get one of these colors:

QBColor	Color	QBColor	Color
0	Black	8	Gray
1	Blue	9	Bright blue
2	Green	10	Bright green
3	Cyan	11	Bright cyan
4	Red	12	Bright red
5	Violet	13	Bright violet
6	Orange	14	Yellow
7	Gray-white	15	Bright white

As the DrawButton_Click code demonstrates, you can use **QBColor**(*number*) in an actual graphics statement. Alternatively, you can define a variable to represent the color and use the variable instead.

Pset draws a point. If you look closely at the program that you just ran, you see a red dot in the center of the green circle.

The **Circle** statement can be complex. With this statement, you can produce the following shapes:

A simple circle: `Circle (xc, yc), radius, color`

An arc: `Circle (xc, yc), radius, color, startangle, endangle`

An ellipse: `Circle (xc, yc), radius, color, , , y/x ratio`

(xc, yc) is the center of the circle. The angles in the **Circle** expression must be in radians. At the start of your program, define `pi = 3.1415926`. You measure angles counterclockwise from the right, which is zero degrees. A 90 degree angle is `pi / 2`; halfway around the circle is pi; all the way around is `2 * pi`.[3] If you make any of the angles negative, the computer draws a line from that end point of the arc to the center. Therefore, if you make both angles negative, you get a wedge.

For ovals (ellipses), you specify the ratio of vertical height to horizontal height. Notice that this ratio comes after you specify the start and end angles. Therefore, if you are not stating these angles, because you want a complete ellipse rather than an arc, you must still leave a space (a comma) as a place holder for the missing angle numbers.

Figure 14-2 illustrates that graphical elements drawn on the form appear *behind* the form's objects.

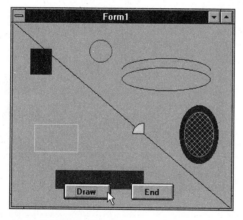

Figure 14-2
Shapes drawn on the form

You can draw on the form, in a picture box, or on printed output.

---

[3]In general, if `angle` is the angle in degrees, the angle in radians, `piangle`, is `piangle = angle / 180 * pi`, where `pi` is the number defined earlier as 3.1415926.

Application 14 **A**llowing the user to draw **A**with the mouse

Overview

The user can select to draw a line, a box, or a circle, positioning and sizing each with the mouse.

Learning Objectives

- handling mouse events
- using scroll bars, check boxes, and picture boxes
- adding simple graphics elements
- using FillColor and AutoRedraw

Instructions

Figure 14-3 shows this application's form. As usual, it includes a label for the title. Down the right are five command buttons: BoxButton, CircleButton, LineButton, EraseButton, and QuitButton. In the center is a picture box with control name Picture1. The default control name seems appropriate, so use it. Across the bottom are two check boxes, a scroll bar, and two labels. The check boxes are named Freeze and Fill. The scroll bar has the maximum value of 15. The empty label in the corner is called Sample, and has its border set to 1 (fixed single).

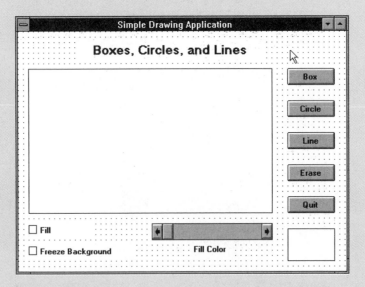

Figure 14-3
The form for a simple drawing application

In the form's general declarations section, set up these five variables as common to all procedures in the form:

```
Dim x1, x2, y1, y2, figure As Integer
```

When the form loads, define some initial settings:

```
Sub Form_Load ()
    Hscroll1.max = 15           ' In case not set at
        design time
    Picture1.ForeColor = 0      ' Set ForeColor.
    Picture1.FillColor = 0      ' Set FillColor.
    Picture1.AutoRedraw = True 'Remember what is drawn
    Sample.BackColor = 0        ' Black
    Picture1.ScaleMode = 3
End Sub
```

The command buttons have very little code:

```
Sub EraseButton_Click ()
    figure = 0
    x1 = 0: x2 = 0: y1 = 0: y2 = 0
    Picture1.Cls
End Sub


Sub BoxButton_Click ()
    figure = 1
End Sub


Sub CircleButton_Click ()
    figure = 2
End Sub


Sub BoxButton_Click ()
    figure = 3
End Sub


Sub LineButton_Click ()
    figure = 3
End Sub


Sub QuitButton_Click ()
    End
End Sub
```

The check boxes toggle the AutoRedraw value between **True** and **False**, and the FillStyle property between 0 and 1:

```
Sub Freeze_Click ()
    Picture1.AutoRedraw = -1 - Picture1.AutoRedraw
        'toggle: 0, -1
End Sub
```

```
Sub Fill_Click ()
    Picture1.FillStyle = 1 - Picture1.FillStyle ⇒
      'toggle: 0, 1
End Sub
```

Note the subtle difference between the two toggle routines. AutoRedraw switches between True, which has the value −1, and False, which has the value 0. To do this, you use a statement of the following form:

```
x = -1 - x.
```

If this is hard to remember, you can always use the following form:

```
If x = True Then x = False Else x = True
```

The FillStyle values are toggling between +1 and zero:

```
x = 1 - x
```

The scroll bar enables the user to select colors:

```
Sub HScroll1_Change ()
    Picture1.FillColor = QBColor(HScroll1.value) 'Set ⇒
      FillColor.
    Sample.BackColor = QBColor(HScroll1.Value) ⇒
      'Display sample color
End Sub
```

You use three mouse events when the user clicks, moves, or releases the mouse while inside the picture area:

```
Sub Picture1_MouseDown (Button As Integer, Shift As ⇒
  Integer, x As Single, y As Single)
    If Button = 1 Then
        x1 = x    'current mouse position
        y1 = y
        If figure = 3 Then Pset (x1, y1), QBColor(0) ⇒
          'start the line
    End If
End Sub


Sub Picture1_MouseMove (Button As Integer, Shift As ⇒
  Integer, x As Single, y As Single)
    If Button = 1 Then
        Select Case figure
          Case 1
            If x2 Or y2 Then    'short for ⇒
              "If x2 <> 0 Or y2 <> 0"
```

```
                                    Picture1.Line (x1, y1)-(x2, y2), ⇒
                                       QBColor(15), B
                    End If
                       'Save current mouse coordinates
                    x2 = x
                    y2 = y
                       'draw the rectangle
                    Picture1.Line (x1, y1)-(x2, y2), ⇒
                       QBColor(0),B
                Case 2            'draw a circle
                    If x2 Or y2 Then 'draw the moving circle
                        If x2 <> x1 Then
                            r = Sqr((x2 - x1) ^ 2 + (y2 - y1)⇒
                               ^ 2)     'Pythagorus
                            Picture1.Circle (x1, y1), r, ⇒
                            QBColor (15) 'erase it
                        End If
                    End If
                    'Save current mouse coordinates
                    x2 = x
                    y2 = y
                                   'draw the final circle
                    If x2 <> x1 Then
                        r = Sqr((x2 - x1) ^ 2 + (y2 - y1) ^ 2)
                        Picture1.Circle (x1, y1), r, QBColor(0)
                    End If
                Case 3            'draw a line
                    Picture1.Line (x1, y1)-(x, y), QBColor(0)
                    x1 = x: y1 = y      'Save mouse coordinates
                Case Else
                    x1 = 0: x2 = 0: y1 = 0: y2 = 0
            End Select
        End If
End Sub


Sub Picture1_MouseUp (Button As Integer, Shift As ⇒
    Integer, x As Single, y As Single)
    If Button = 1 Then    'left button was let go
        'draw the shape in its final position
        Select Case figure
            Case 1
                Picture1.Line (x1, y1)-(x2, y2), ⇒
                   QBColor(0), B
            Case 2
                r = Sqr((x2 - x1) ^ 2 + (y2 - y1) ^ 2)
                Picture1.Circle (x1, y1), r, QBColor(0)
            Case 3
```

```
                    Picture1.Line -(x, y), QBColor(0)
             Case Else
        End Select
        x1 = 0 'clear out the variables ready for next shape
        y1 = 0
        x2 = 0
        y2 = 0
        figure = 0
    End If
End Sub
```

To enlarge the circles and boxes, the program draws over the old figure in white and draws the figure in its new position. The program stores the old coordinates as x1 and y1, and the new coordinates are x2 and y2. When the user moves large sections of graphics, the process becomes a little erratic. And sometimes a little bit of a shrinking filled box or circle gets left behind. One of the modifications deals with this problem.

The outlines of the growing figures damage the background of previously drawn figures. This damage occurs because before drawing a circle or rectangle in a new position, the program erases it from its old position by drawing the figure in the background white color. Unfortunately, that erasing can remove part of a previously drawn figure. In "real" paint programs, however, an outline of a growing box or circle passes safely over the background without leaving tracks. You can see this for yourself with Visual Basic as you design your forms. Nondestructive movement of a line across a background is quite difficult to accomplish in QBasic code. But if the Visual Basic programmer's interface can do it, the code must be in there somewhere. In fact, there is a Visual Basic and Windows routine that can move or resize a rectangle safely. Accessing such an application program interface (API) requires techniques that are beyond the scope of this book.

Experiment with the AutoRedraw feature by clicking in the Freeze Background check box. With Picture1.AutoRedraw on (–1, or **True**), Visual Basic keeps a record in memory of what to display in Picture1. Erase the screen with and without the Freeze Background check box selected. While the program runs, try minimizing the application (parking it at the bottom of the screen) and bringing it back. What does AutoRedraw protect?

Modifications

1. Try to get rid of the remnants of shrinking filled boxes and circles. For a circle, instead of erasing the large circle and redrawing the smaller circle, you could erase (draw in white) a series of circles with increasingly smaller radii until you reach the smaller circle. Or you might set FillColor to white when you draw your large circle (to erase it) and then reset FillColor to its proper value when you draw the new circle.

2. In Chapter 6, you used three scroll bars and the **RGB()** function to give you millions of colors. You might add two other scroll bars to give the program this capacity.

3. The program draws all figures in black, regardless of FillColor. Try drawing with the FillColor. To do so requires only a simple change.

4. Did you define a variable to use in the appropriate places so that you didn't have to keep referring to HScroll1.Value?

Enhancement

An interesting effect is a field of random stars. Make a button called Stars that will display a random star field. In a loop, depending on the number of stars that you want, pick random x values ranging between 1 and Picture1's width. For example, if the width is 3000, a statement such as the following would create a random x position for a star:

```
x = Int( Rnd * 3000 + 1)
```

Pick a random y value for your stars, scaled to Picture1's height. Then use **Pset** to draw a black dot at that location (or, better, a white dot against a black background). Make a button called Stars. You can also enable the user to determine the number of stars.

Exercises

At your desk

1. Distinguish between the form's Width and its ScaleWidth. Which affects the actual size of the form on the screen?

2. What property of the form determines the type of pattern that appears when a box or circle is filled?

3. The following box represents a form whose coordinate system goes from (0, 0) to (1000, 1000). What would appear on the form after you execute the following commands?

```
Line (100, 500) - (100, 800)
Line (10, 10)-(900, 20), QBColor(0),BF
Circle (800,200),50
```

4. Since each color produced by the **RGB()** function is constructed from red, green, and blue variables that range from 0 to 255, excactly how many possible colors are there?

At your computer

On an empty form, draw the pattern shown in Figure 14-4. It requires three **Line** statements and a Circle statement. The inner box actually consists of two boxes: a brightly colored box drawn on top of its black "shadow," and a box two pixels to the right and down. Set ScaleWidth and ScaleHeight in Form_Load. Put the drawing routine in Form_Paint.

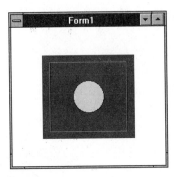

Figure 14-4
A pattern of boxes and a circle

Run the program and try resizing the form with your mouse. Minimize the program (click on the down arrow to park the running program as an icon at the bottom of the screen). What icon do you see?

Now add your ScaleWidth and ScaleHeight lines to Form_Resize, followed by the following code:

```
Cls        'clear the screen
Form_Paint  'paint the screen again (i.e. call the ⇒
  Form_Paint routine)
```

Now see what happens when you resize the form while the program runs. What does the icon look like when you minimize the form?

Notice the difference between the way that the boxes and the circle attempt to maintain their horizontal and vertical scales independently. Does the circle become an ellipse?

To see an interesting optical illusion, reverse the colors of the inner box so that the shadow is higher to the left (as would be the case if the light source were from the lower right). Do your eyes accept the illusion that the object is being illuminated from below?

Programming Adventure 3

Concentration Game

In this programming adventure, you create a fully playable version of a traditional memory game.

Overview

The user selects a one- or two-player game. The computer displays a game board that contains 20 closed windows. The program hides 10 pairs of pictures randomly. The player attempts to find matching pictures by selecting two windows with the mouse.

Learning Objectives

- loading pictures into picture boxes
- randomizing
- drawing lines
- enabling, disabling, showing, and hiding controls
- using more than one form
- using frames
- using option buttons
- restarting a program
- using arrays

Instructions

For this application, you draw two forms. The first is the main game board, and the second is an introductory screen with option buttons.

The main form (shown in Figure PA3.1) has the dimensions 7,485 by 6,225. It contains nine labels, two buttons, a timer, and a frame that contains 20 picture boxes.

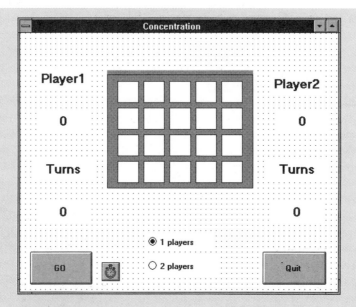

Figure PA3-1
The form for the main game board

This form provides a great exercise in making control arrays, because you pair each label down the left side with its corresponding label on the other side. After making the label for the title, make a label called PlayerLabel, containing the caption Player1. Specify the FontSize as 13.5 and the Alignment as 2 (centered). Then choose the Edit menu's Copy and Paste commands. When asked whether you want a control array, answer Yes. This gives you two similar labels: PlayerLabel(0) on the left and PlayerLabel(1) on the right. Do the same for the other labels. Call them, going from top to bottom, MatchBox, TurnsLabel, and TurnsBox. In each case, first make the one on the left, choose the Copy and Paste commands, and drag the duplicate to its new location on the right.

Next make a 3,375-by-2,655 frame. Erase the caption and pick an interesting BackColor.

The next part is tricky. Make the first picture box 495 by 495. Make its control name Square. Copy it, but *click on the frame before pasting it.* If you don't select the frame first, the pasted picture goes into the first picture rather than into the frame.

Answer Yes when asked whether to make each picture box a control array, and continue until you have 20 picture boxes. The first has the index 0 and the last one index 19. Therefore, you have a control array of picture boxes: Square(0), Square(1), Square(2), and so on up to Square(19).

Create the two buttons. The code for the Quit button requires that you make a second form. Leave that until later. Here is the code for the Go button:

```
Sub GoButton_Click ()
    Randomize Timer   'makes a different random setup ⇒
       each time
```

```
    For i = 0 To 19        'shuffle the pictures
        j = Int(Rnd * 20)
        t$ = pict(i): pict(i) = pict(j): pict(j) = t$
    Next i

    For i = 0 To 19        'put the pictures in the squares
        Square(i).picture = LoadPicture(pict(i))
        Square(i).Enabled = True
    Next i

    For i = 0 To 19        'draw the doors closing
        For j = 1 To 610
            Square(i).Line (0, j)-(695, j), RGB(255, 0, 0)
        Next j
    Next i

    If Option1.Value = True Then    'one-player game ⇒
        was selected
        players = 1
                                'turn of player 2's info
        PlayerLabel(1).Visible = False
        MatchBox(1).Visible = False
        TurnsLabel(1).Visible = False
        TurnsBox(1).Visible = False
    Else
        players = 2
    End If

    GoButton.Visible = False        'turn off Go and ⇒
        Option buttons
    Option1.Visible = False
    Option2.Visible = False

    player = Int(Rnd * players)     'pick random ⇒
        starting player
    EnablePlayer                    'turn on that player's info
End Sub
```

The preceding code refers to an array pict( ). This array holds the names of the pictures that load into each square. To set up the array, you must do two things. First, you must declare pict( ) and the other common variables. Click on the form and enter the following in the general declarations window:

```
Dim selected(20) As Integer
Dim pict(20) As String
Dim player As Integer
Dim players As Integer
Dim picked As Integer
Dim firstpick, secondpick As Integer
Dim matches(1)
Dim turns(1)
```

The second step is to give the **pict( )** array actual values. Define them in Form_Load:

```
Sub Form_Load ()
   For j = 0 To 1
      pict(0 + j) = "\vb\icons\computer\disk01.ico"
      pict(2 + j) = "\vb\icons\computer\disk02.ico"
      pict(4 + j) = "\vb\icons\computer\disk03.ico"
      pict(6 + j) = "\vb\icons\computer\mac01.ico"
      pict(8 + j) = "\vb\icons\computer\drive01.ico"
      pict(10 + j) = "\vb\icons\computer\pc01.ico"
      pict(12 + j) = "\vb\icons\computer\monitr01.ico"
      pict(14 + j) = "\vb\icons\computer\mouse01.ico"
      pict(16 + j) = "\vb\icons\computer\key02.ico"
      pict(18 + j) = "\vb\icons\computer\key03.ico"
   Next
   Option1.Value = True
   Option1.Visible = True
   Option2.Visible = True
   GoButtonVisible = True
   For i = 0 To 19
      Square(i).Enabled = False
   Next i
   For i = 0 To 1
      matches(i) = 0: turns(i) = 0
   Next i
   player = 0 : Timer1.Enabled = False
End Sub
```

Form_Load assigns the same picture to two different **pict( )** arrays. The preceding code refers to icons that come with Visual Basic and are stored in a \VB\ICONS\COMPUTER directory. If you don't have that directory, you have to find some icons or draw some small pictures. (The disks accompanying this book include these icons.)

The GoButton_Click code refers to EnablePlayer. This is code that you will use twice, so put it in a general subprocedure by typing **Sub** EnablePlayer in any code window. Enter these statements:

```
Sub EnablePlayer
   nonplayer = 1 - player
   PlayerLabel(player).Enabled = True
   PlayerLabel(nonplayer).Enabled = False
   MatchBox(player).Enabled = True
   MatchBox(nonplayer).Enabled = False
   TurnsLabel(player).Enabled = True
   TurnsLabel(nonplayer).Enabled = False
   TurnsBox(player).Enabled = True
   TurnsBox(nonplayer).Enabled = False
End Sub
```

Now enter the routine that executes when the user selects a square by clicking on it:

```
Sub square_Click (Index As Integer)
    Select Case picked
        Case 0
            Square(Index).picture = ⇒
                LoadPicture(pict(Index))
            picked = 1
            firstpick = Index
        Case 1
            Square(Index).picture = ⇒
                LoadPicture(pict(Index))
            secondpick = Index
            Timer1.Enabled = True
            picked = 2
        Case Else
    End Select
End Sub
```

The user plays the game by clicking on two boxes. The variable `picked` stands for the number of boxes currently selected, either 0, 1, or 2 boxes. The **LoadPicture** statement brings the picture into the appropriate square, as defined by the value of Index (which the computer controls). You store the index in the variables `firstpicked` and `secondpicked`. These variables are used by the timer routine, which starts when the user selects a second square.

Here's the timer code:

```
Timer1_Timer()
    picked = 0
    Timer1.Enabled = False              'turn off the timer
    turns(player) = turns(player) + 1   'increase the ⇒
        turn counter
    TurnsBox(player).caption = Str$(turns(player))

    If pict(firstpick) = pict(secondpick) Then    'it's ⇒
        a match
        Beep
        matches(player) = matches(player) + 1
        MatchBox(player).caption = Str$(matches(player))
    Else
                                        'close the doors
        For j = 1 To 610
            Square(firstpick).Line (0, j)-(695, j),
                RGB(255, 0, 0)
            Square(secondpick).Line (0, j)-(695, j),
                RGB(255, 0, 0)
        Next j
                            'switch players if 2 person game
        If players = 2 Then player = 1 - player
```

```
                        EnablePlayer
                End If
                totalmatches = matches(player) + matches(1 - player)
                If totalmatches = 10 Then      'every door is now ⇒
                  picked
                    form2.caption = "Game Over"
                    form2.ContinueButton.Visible = False  'hide ⇒
                      continue button
                    QuitButton_click      'jump to form1's QuitButton⇒
                      routine
                    totalmatches = 0        'reset for possible new game
                End If
        End Sub
```

The timer's countdown begins when the user selects a second square. Make
Timer1.Interval = 1000. This produces a one-second pause before the timer shuts
the windows. The Timer1_Timer routine also updates the scoreboard, checks for
a winner, and switches players.

The second form (see Figure PA3-2) pops up when the user clicks on Form1's
Quit button.

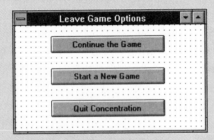

Figure PA3-2
The application's second form

Place this form below the game board on the screen so that it doesn't overlap any
pictures. *(To see why, when you finish coding the game, try overlapping the game board
and press Continue.)* Make the control names for the form's three buttons
ContinueButton, NewButton, and QuitConButton.

You want to make the new form pop up when the user clicks on Form1's Quit
button:

```
Sub QuitButton_Click ()
    form2.Show 1        ' start leave options form
    'program returns here when form2 is closed
    form2.Hide  'turn off form2
    form1.Show  'turn on form1
    Form1.Enabled = True    'make it active again
End Sub
```

Notice the first line in the preceding routine. The 1 specifies a modal form, which must be closed before the user can access any control on another form; that is, all controls on other forms are disabled. You could achieve the same effect by setting Form1.Enabled to **False**.

Here is the code for the three buttons on Form2:

```
Sub NewButton
    form2.Hide
End Sub

Sub ContinueButton
    form2.Hide
    Unload form2
    Unload form1
    Load form1
End Sub

Sub QuitConButton
    End
End Sub
```

You now are ready to play the game.

Modifications

1. Change the color of the active player's statistics to red, then black again when the player's turn is over.

2. When the user clicks on the Go button, make a label appear that announces which player will start first.

Appendix I Creating an Icon for Your Application on Your Windows Desktop

In Chapter 1, you learned that after creating a Visual Basic application, you can turn it into a stand-alone .EXE file. That is, you can turn your application into a file that does not require Visual Basic to run. This appendix reviews the required steps for doing so.

The result will be an .EXE file on your disk. The final step is to add this file to Program Manager. Then you can run the executable program by clicking on its icon on your Windows desktop.

AI.1 Choosing an icon for your application

Your form has an Icon property. You can change the built-in icon from the default icon (shown in Figure AI-1) to another icon. Click on the ellipsis (the three periods or dots) at the right of the Settings box in the properties list. The dialog box that appears enables you to choose any icon that you can find on your drive. Many .ICO files come with Visual Basic. You can also change to your Windows directory and select an icon from PROGMAN.EXE or MORICONS.DLL.

Figure AI-1
Choosing the default icon from the Properties window

AI.2 Making the executable file

From the Visual Basic menu, choose File and then Make EXE File. The Make EXE File dialog box opens asking for a name, drive, and directory for the .EXE file (see Figure AI-2). The default directory will probably be your Visual Basic directory. On your own computer, you would probably place your application in a subdirectory that contains a related application. Or, if you intend to give your application to someone else, you could make the .EXE file on your A drive.

Suppose that you call your executable file FIRSTONE.EXE and place it on the root directory of your C drive, as shown in Figure AI-2. Click on OK to create an executable file called C:\FIRSTONE.EXE.

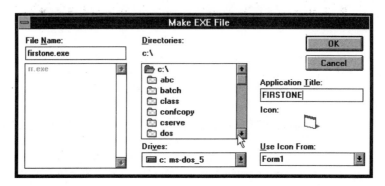

Figure AI-2
Naming your .EXE file

You can distribute this file freely. Recipients do not need to have Visual Basic to run your application. They must, however, have the file VBRUN300.DLL (or VBRUN200.DLL or VBRUN100.DLL if you are using an earlier version of Visual Basic) in their WINDOWS subdirectory. This file comes with Visual Basic and you can distribute it along with your application.

AI.3 Creating a Program Manager icon for your executable file

Leave or minimize Visual Basic and look at your Program Manager window. Although the file that you just created is on your drive, you do not see it in Program Manager. To add the program's icon to a group on your desktop, first click open the group, open the File menu, and choose New. You then see the New Program Object dialog box shown in Figure AI-3.

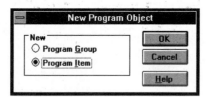

Figure AI-3
Adding an item to a Program Manager group

With the Program Item option selected, click on OK. You then see the Program Item Properties dialog box shown in Figure AI-4.

```
┌─────────────────────────────────────────────────────┐
│ ⊖                 Program Item Properties             │
├─────────────────────────────────────────────────────┤
│  Description:      ┌─────────────────────┐  ┌───────┐ │
│                    │ First VB Program    │  │  OK   │ │
│  Command Line:     ┌─────────────────────┐  └───────┘ │
│                    │ c:\firstone.exe     │  ┌───────┐ │
│  Working Directory:┌─────────────────────┐  │Cancel │ │
│                    │ c:\                 │  └───────┘ │
│  Shortcut Key:     ┌─────────────────────┐           │
│                    │ None              · │  ┌───────┐ │
│                    └─────────────────────┘  │Browse.│ │
│                    ☐ Run Minimized          └───────┘ │
│                                          ┌──────────┐ │
│                                          │Change Icon│ │
│                                          └──────────┘ │
│                                          ┌──────────┐ │
│                                          │   Help   │ │
│                                          └──────────┘ │
└─────────────────────────────────────────────────────┘
```

Figure AI-4
Setting your application's name and startup instructions

The information in the Command Line text box assumes that you placed your
.EXE file in the root directory of drive C. If you store your FIRSTONE.EXE
application in some other directory, your Command Line will differ. You might
have to browse to find it.

Appendix II Pasting Help Screen Code into Your Application

In Chapter 3, you learned how to access Visual Basic's Help screens. In these screens, you can search for information about a concept, technique, or Visual Basic command. Many of the pages that appear in response to your inquiry contain examples that demonstrate how to use the command in your program. This appendix presents the steps for copying and pasting portions of the Visual Basic Help screen examples into your program.

InputBox is a Visual Basic command that displays a small window that prompts the user to enter some data. Suppose that you are looking for information on how to use **InputBox**.

First open the Help menu and choose Search. In the Search dialog box, select or enter **InputBox**, as shown in Figure AII-1.

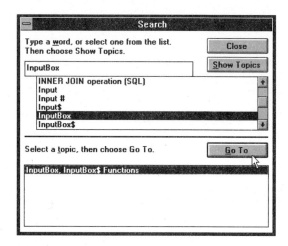

Figure AII-1
Find InputBox in the Search dialog box

Choose the Go To button. You then see the Help screen shown in Figure AII.2. The Help information indicates that **InputBox** has an example. To see it, just point to the word Example, as shown in Figure AII.2. Your mouse arrow becomes a finger graphic. Click the mouse button.

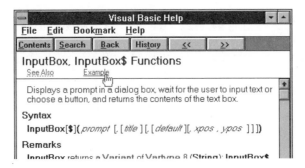

Figure AII-2
Point to the word Example

After you click on Example, you see the example window shown in Figure AII-3. The example provides an actual **Sub** that uses **InputBox**. Instructions tell you how to add the example to your program. In this case, the example appears in **Sub** Form_Click.

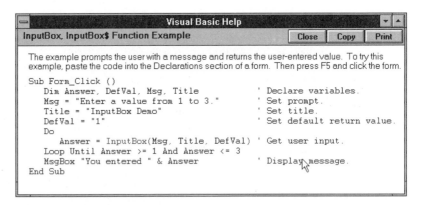

Figure AII-3
The InputBox example window

Click on the Copy button. This brings up the example's Copy window, as shown in Figure AII-4. Highlight the lines of code and choose Copy.

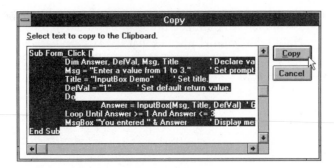

Figure AII-4
The copy window with code highlighted

You can now exit Help. Then click on your form to bring up the form's code window. Follow the instructions at the top of the example, which were, in this case, to place the code into the general declarations.

When you run the program and click on the form, you see the result of the **InputBox** code, as shown in Figure AII-5.

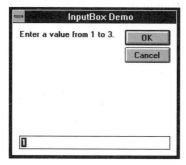

Figure AII-5
An InputBox window

Incidently, the **InputBox** example includes a logical bug. Clicking on the Cancel button brings up the error message shown in Figure AII-6.

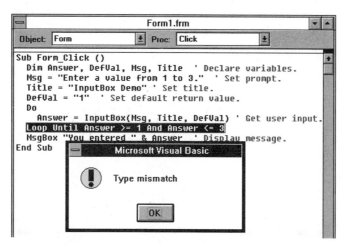

Figure AII-6
Clicking on the Cancel button causes the program to stop

The explanation is that clicking on Cancel causes answer to be a nil string (a pair of double quotation marks with nothing between them). The **Loop Until** statement tries to evaluate a nil string, which is impossible. You should check for this condition. For example, immediately before the **Loop Until** statement, you could insert the following:

```
If answer = "" Then MsgBox "You pressed Cancel": End
```

Index

In addition to being discussed in the text, many of the concepts, statements, and controls listed in this index appear in the examples of code throughout the book. The examples of code that are listed in the index have been chosen because they illustrate the topic clearly; not every example of code is included. Page numbers followed by an "f" indicate that the reference appears in a footnote.